HEARING MARK

HEARING MARK

A Listener's Guide

Elizabeth Struthers Malbon

TRINITY PRESS INTERNATIONAL
Harrisburg, Pennsylvania

Trinity Press International, P.O. Box 1321, Harrisburg, PA 17105
Trinity Press International is a division of The Morehouse Group.

Cover art: *San Marco,* Gino Severini. Photo by Vatican Museums.

Cover design: Wesley Hoke

Library of Congress Cataloging-in-Publication Data

Malbon, Elizabeth Struthers.
  Hearing Mark : a listener's guide / Elizabeth Struthers Malbon.
    p. cm.
Includes bibliographical references.
  ISBN 1-56338-379-9 (pbk. : alk. paper)
  1. Bible. N.T. Mark—Commentaries. I. Title.
BS2585.53 .M35 2002
226.3'07—dc21
                                                              2002001554

An online study guide is available at www.trinitypressintl.com.

Printed in the United States of America

        04 05 06 07   10 9 8 7 6 5 4 3 2

Dedicated with thanks to

Dr. Robert A. Spivey
Former President, Randolph Macon Woman's College
(formerly Professor of Religion at Florida State University)
who introduced me to the academic study of the Gospel of Mark

Dr. John R. Donahue, S.J.
Raymond E. Brown Distinguished Professor of New Testament Studies,
St. Mary's Seminary and University
(formerly Professor at the Vanderbilt Divinity School)
who introduced me to the Greek text of Mark and its scholarly literature

The Rt. Rev. Martin G. Townsend
Bishop, Episcopal Diocese of Easton (Maryland), retired
(formerly Rector of Christ Church, Blacksburg, Virginia)
who introduced me to the congregational reading of Mark's Gospel

Contents

Acknowledgments

This book has not come into being in isolation but in community. Four communities have been of special significance thus far. Those of you who are reading this now form the fifth.

Scholars will recognize the unnamed community of those whose books and articles I have read, whose scholarly papers I have heard, and with whom I have enjoyed lively conversations at professional meetings. I hope these readers will sense in my virtual footnotes appreciation for their collegiality. Without them this book could not have been written, yet it is not written for them.

This listener's guide to Mark's Gospel is written for laity in Christian churches, and I am happy to acknowledge the encouragement I received from a community of such listeners—the second community in the formation of this book—when I gave four talks on "Hearing the Gospel of Mark" during Lent in the year 2000. Six congregations in Blacksburg, Virginia, joined together for the event: Blacksburg Baptist Church, Blacksburg Presbyterian Church, Blacksburg United Methodist Church, Christ Episcopal Church, Luther Memorial Lutheran Church, and St. Mary's Roman Catholic Church. I am grateful to Clare Fisher-Davies, rector of Christ Church, for the initial invitation and to Elizabeth Foster for recording the presentations. At a performance of Mark's Gospel at the close of the series, an offering was collected for Habitat for Humanity. In thanksgiving for the community of Blacksburg, I am pledging a tithe of the royalties from this guide to this agency, whose goals include strengthening community and communities.

Third, I am especially pleased to name an implicit community of seven readers of a complete (but not quite final) draft of the manuscript for this book. These women and men represent a variety of interests and professions (college president, preschool teacher, plumber, professor, priest). Each of these readers was generous in giving time and energy to help me communicate more clearly with my unknown readers. Among the seven were the three persons to whom this book is dedicated, although the dedication was based on their earlier contributions to my development as a listener to Mark's Gospel. Each of these three has offered a range of comments, but I am especially indebted to Robert Spivey for careful stylistic comments, to John Donahue for thoughtful pastoral comments, and to Martin Townsend for engaging exegetical (interpretive) comments. Readers Laurie Shepherd and David Bernard each helped me see things I had not seen; I am thankful to them, but not surprised. Laurie has often recommended books to me from her own broad reading, and David has acted out his passionate concern for Christians today who share the experience of suffering with Mark's first audience. Clare Fisher-Davies offered lovely suggestions I wish I'd thought of and exuberant promises to borrow material for sermons. All of these readers I have known for a number of years—in some cases a large number! Philip Ruge-Jones and I have met once, sitting on the floor in a crowded room at a professional meeting, listening to a scholarly paper about how first-century readers would have heard Mark's Gospel. I am grateful for the generous and important help his comments have provided in relation to our common interest in Mark as a heard story. All seven readers claimed to have enjoyed their work, and the seven baskets full of comments they shared with me were a delightful feast indeed.

Finally, I acknowledge with gratitude the community of editors at Trinity Press International, especially Henry Carrigan (editorial director), Laura Hudson (managing editor), Mark Siemens (copyeditor), and Wesley Hoke (cover designer), who smoothed the final transition of this material, which—like Mark's Gospel in this respect—began orally, was reduced to writing, and lastly was produced as a book in order to reach out to a broader community.

CREDITS

The map on page 36 is reprinted from my *Narrative Space and Mythic Meaning in Mark* (Sheffield, England: Sheffield Academic Press, 1991) by permission of the publisher.

Nearly all quotations from the Gospel of Mark are my own translations, made from the third edition of the Greek text published by the United Bible Societies and edited by Kurt Aland and others, copyright © 1975. Note, however, that often I am paraphrasing or creatively retelling, not directly quoting.

All quotations from other biblical books are from the New Revised Standard Version of the Bible, copyright © 1989 by the Division of Christian Education of the National Council of the Churches of Christ in the U.S.A. Occasional Markan quotations from the NRSV are marked as such.

Assumptions

This book seeks to help you read—and especially hear—the Gospel of Mark more perceptively and more powerfully. But before I focus on our role in reading and hearing, I need to make explicit six simple assumptions I hold about the author's role in writing. If we differ significantly on these assumptions about how the Gospel of Mark was written, we may find we also have quite different perspectives concerning how Mark is to be read, heard, and interpreted. Even if we agree on these assumptions, we are likely to have some degree of disagreement on interpretation because we bring different resources with us to the process of reading, hearing, and understanding. That's okay—even good. None of us is the final authority on these matters. The Gospel of Mark has held up very well under differing interpretations for nearly two thousand years. And it is with that period of two thousand years that I begin my list of six assumptions about how the Gospel of Mark was written.

Assumption 1: The Gospel of Mark was written long ago.

That is pretty obvious. But isn't it true that we don't usually think about anything in the Bible as being written long ago because we are interested in the meaning it has for us today? Yet it is good to remind ourselves that Mark's Gospel was originally written long ago—around 70 of the Common Era (C.E., a more neutral, scholarly designation than A.D.). Most scholars agree that Mark was the first Gospel written and that later Gospel writers had access to Mark and used it as the basis for new versions for different communities—the Gospels of Matthew and Luke. We know that a significant event took place in the year 70: the destruction of the Jewish temple in Jerusalem by the Romans. It appears that the Gospel of Mark was written either in anticipation of or in response to that event, maybe right before or right after. I think right after. In either case, we agree Mark was written quite a long time ago. This means that all the shared assumptions of Mark's author and his audience may not be known to us. Just as there is an archaeology of physical remains from the first century, there is and must be an archaeology of first-century texts.

Assumption 2: The Gospel of Mark was written far away.

It was written in and for a culture different from our own. It was written in the Greek language, not Plato's Greek but the Greek made common among the peoples of the eastern Mediterranean by the conquests and influence of Alexander the Great. You've heard the phrase, "A lot gets lost in translation"? Well, if you have a document that was written that long ago and that far away in a different language, a lot can get lost! There's plenty of room here for cultural gaps, for misunderstanding. Or, put more positively, if we learn more about the context of origin, there's plenty of room for increased understanding, for more meaningful interpretations of the Gospel of Mark. To be sure, the text touches us from across the millennia and from across the continents, but increased understanding comes not in ignoring this distance in time and space but in attending to it.

Many scholars think that Mark's Gospel was written in Rome. The memory of Peter was venerated very early in Rome, and Peter has an important role to play in Mark. Other scholars think it may have been written in Syria. We will probably never know for sure, and it may not matter that much for our hearing of the Gospel. The main thing to realize is that there is a cultural gap between what we call the world behind the text, the world of Jesus and the evangelist (the Gospel's author), and our world, the world in front of the text. The more we appreciate and understand that gap the better we can bridge it. Scholars can provide some bridge-building comments. If it's helpful to read comments and notes for understanding sixteenth-century Shakespeare, if it's essential to read comments and notes for deciphering eighth-century *Beowulf,* surely it makes sense to explore some cultural commentary when reading Mark's Gospel, written nearly two millennia ago and half a world away.

Assumption 3: The Gospel of Mark was written anonymously.

I frequently surprise students with this statement. "No, no," they say. "Right at the top of the page in my Bible it says 'The Gospel according to Mark.'" That is true; it does have that heading at the top of the page. For almost all of the Gospel's life it's had that heading, but probably not for the first one hundred years or so. It's quite surprising that all four Gospels seem to be about a generation or maybe a hundred years older than their names. There's nothing in the text of Mark (which starts at 1:1) that mentions an author. We do have Eusebius, a fourth-century church historian, telling us that he read something by Papias (whose documents we don't have anymore), writing in the second century, who said that Mark was the interpreter of Peter. Unfortunately, Eusebius also says elsewhere that one can't trust Papias! So I don't know about that. But that's the best documentation we have: Eusebius said in the fourth century that Papias said in the second century that Mark was the interpreter of Peter in the first century. In Greek manuscripts the title is *Kata Markon* (According to Mark). In Latin this is *Secundum Marcum*, as seen on the evangelist's book in Gino Severini's painting on the cover of this guide.

Now I am willing to go with a two-millennium tradition of calling this book the Gospel according to Mark. I am going to call it the Gospel of Mark. I am going to call the author Mark. But when I do so I am following a convention, taking part in a religious tradition, not making a historical judgment based on authenticated information. I am also going to follow the lead of the author. The author apparently felt that the story was more important than the storyteller, so I am going to assume that too. If the author had wanted us to know about himself or herself, then he or she could have written that in. The author wanted us to know about Jesus as the Christ, so that's what we're going to pay attention to.

Assumption 4: The Gospel of Mark was written from faith to faith.

Perhaps this is obvious too, but it is well worth making explicit. The Gospel was not written by a reporter who was seeking to get all "the facts" straight but who did not care about their implications. (In fact, "the facts" is a rather modern concept.) The Gospel was written by someone who believes that Jesus is the Christ, the Son of God, assumes that the audience believes that too, and wants to show the audience how their life together can be deeper and richer—and how their community can move out into the broader world because of that. Mark's Gospel is not written objectively: "I had to write a term paper on something, so I picked Jesus." No, Mark's Gospel is written because the author thinks Jesus and his followers are turning the world upside down. It's a good news sermon. When I tell my students that Mark's Gospel is a sermon, I find that some of them have apparently been hearing a lot of bad news sermons. They think a sermon is a lecture telling you what you did wrong and what you should do to be an acceptable person. Mark's Gospel is a sermon that proclaims the good news. That kind of sermon tells you something good that God is doing in the world. The Gospel is not a simple history book. And it's not neutral. It's written from the persuaded to be persuasive.

Assumption 5: The Gospel of Mark was written as a story.

It's not a list of theological propositions: (1) Jesus is the Christ, (2) Jesus is the Son of God, and so on. And it's not a list of personality traits: (1) Jesus is compassionate, (2) Jesus is able to attract followers, and so on. It's not even a list of events: (1) Jesus is baptized, (2) Jesus calms the sea, . . . , although the term "events" does bring us closer to what it is as a story. A story involves characters interacting in a plot of interconnected events, set in certain times and places. The characters are the who, the settings are the where and when, the plot is the how and why. The rhetoric—or various means of persuasion, including such things as foreshadowing, parallelism, allusions, and symbolic language—also contributes to the how and why. To recognize that Mark's Gospel was written as a story does not answer the question of its historical accuracy; stories may be historical, fictional, or historical fiction—although this categorization is anachronistic when applied to first-century texts. Application of twenty-first-century standards of historical accuracy to Mark's Gospel is not the goal here, but rather appreciation of the narrative nature of the text.

Stories would have come naturally to Mark and his first-century audience. The first believers in Jesus as the Christ were Jewish; the Bible of the early Christians was the Jewish Bible in its Greek translation (the Septuagint); and the Bible is full of stories—stories about how God acts and how the people of God act in response. Perhaps Greek philosophers worried about the essence of God, but Jewish and Jewish-Christian storytellers focused on the activity of God and God in Christ. In the biblical tradition not only have the people of God imagined their relationship with God as a story, but also individual members continue to experience their own lives as stories. Perhaps this is why it is so easy for us to get caught up in the story Mark's Gospel tells.

Assumption 6: The Gospel of Mark was written to be heard.

Most people in the ancient world couldn't read; maybe 10 percent, give or take, were literate. Perhaps a higher percentage of Jews were readers because reading the Scripture was important. The world was not for readers; the world was for hearers, for listeners. Even those who were readers read out loud to others. And even if you were a reader, you likely couldn't afford books—or even paper. Books were still something of a novelty in the first century; the codex (or book) was just winning out over the scroll, but both were very expensive. Parchment and paper were definitely for the elites. The number of books and amount of paper we have in one household today would have been rich for a town in the ancient world.

So the Gospel was written to be heard—and not in little pieces like we hear it today. We read it silently—in paragraphs or maybe chapters, or we hear it read from the pulpit in church—broken into sections by the lectionary and followed by the sermon. It wasn't meant to be heard that way. It was meant to be heard all together; it was meant to be listened to. So I'll frequently use the term "audience" because that word includes both hearers and readers, with the accent on those who hear. If you have the opportunity to hear the Gospel of Mark read aloud, or recited, or presented dramatically, you will be doing what the first Christians did, gathering—perhaps in a place of worship—to listen to the story, to hear the good news.

So, I am beginning with these six assumptions about the origin of Mark's Gospel. The Gospel of Mark was written

- long ago
- far away
- anonymously
- from faith to faith
- as a story
- to be heard.

These assumptions will, of course, influence how I hear the Gospel and how I retell it for your hearing.

These are some assumptions I hold about the author of Mark's Gospel. Now I'd like to share some assumptions I hold about you as a member of the audience of Mark's Gospel and of this book! Indeed, my title, *Hearing Mark*, and subtitle, *A Listener's Guide*, suggest a link between Mark's first-century audience and you as a twenty-first-century hearer/reader. If none of my assumptions fit you at all, this may not be the book for you! Let's part friends. But if some of what I am assuming about you is appropriate, I hope you will feel ready and eager to begin together.

Assumption 1: You have probably heard or read at least parts of the Gospel of Mark before.

If you have not, a special welcome—it's a great book!

Assumption 2: You have access not only to a copy of the Gospel of Mark but also to the whole Christian Bible in some recent English translation.

Although the New Revised Standard Version is in the near background of my study, here I am actually making my own translation from the Greek text of Mark. Quite frequently I am not even translating at all but freely paraphrasing—or even creatively retelling. The storyteller in Mark has influenced me! But I am assuming you have at hand a careful translation. There are a number of recent English translations; you may have a favorite. It is very helpful to compare different translations. The New Revised Standard Version is frequently used by scholars because it tries to be "as literal as possible, as free as necessary," but the NRSV was commissioned by the National Council of the Churches of Christ in the U.S.A. for reading aloud in churches.

Assumption 3: You have your copy of Mark with you as you are reading this guide and are committed to keeping it with you and stopping to read it regularly as you read through my text, which is entirely secondary to Mark's.

My paraphrasing and retelling is intended to be heard in concert with a standard translation. (I hear the NRSV and RSV in my head.) I would suggest reading the portion of Mark listed in each of my chapter titles before you read that chapter—and perhaps afterwards as well. The chapter and verse references given in headings and subheadings will help you follow along in your Bible as you read this guide.

Assumption 4: You know how to decipher chapter and verse references.

Mark 1–4 means chapters one through four of Mark. Mark 1:1–4 means verses one through four of chapter one of Mark. Mark 1:1–4:1 means from verse one of chapter one through verse one of chapter four. Mark 4:1a means the first part of verse one of chapter four. The chapter and verse references are not original to the Greek text but were added sometime in the Middle Ages, especially to aid manuscript copyists. Thus they do not give us clues to the author's organization, but they are convenient.

Assumption 5: You see yourself in some relationship to the Christian tradition—although it may be a somewhat complex relationship involving questions as well as affirmations.

If you do not see yourself in such a relationship, you will no doubt deal in your own way with the prayers that open and close each of my chapters. The phrases of each prayer suggest the major themes I have drawn from the portion of Mark's Gospel discussed in that chapter. Thus before the chapter each prayer is a preview; afterwards it is a review. In both cases it can be an invitation to meditation.

Assumption 6: You are probably reading this silently and alone (this is the twenty-first century!).

It would be wonderful, however, if you could share what you are reading here and in Mark with others, making sure to listen as well as to speak. (Some additional resources for those who want to learn more about Mark's Gospel or to prepare to listen to its oral presentation are described under the heading "Extras" at the close of this book.) Discussing any text—for example, Mark's or mine—with others makes clear your own important and inevitable role as an interpreter. Not everyone will understand what I write in the same way. Not everyone— certainly not every scholar—understands what Mark wrote in the same way! We can't take the interpreter out of interpretation—and why should we try? Mark's story tries very hard to engage us in its interpretation. I would be disappointed if you received my comments on Mark's Gospel as a closing down of the complexity and creativity Mark opens up. Reading or hearing another's interpretation is not an excuse for avoiding your own but an open invitation to share in the conversation. Mark's Gospel was written for a community—and for community. And so is my book. My book is offered as *a* guide, not *the* guide; a guide may point things out along the way, but the journey is yours.

By now you've probably made some assumptions about me as well. That would be understandable. I'm sure it would help me communicate with you if I could know these assumptions directly. In the meantime, I can tell you three things about me that are of special relevance here.

Item 1: I am a teacher.

This you've probably already picked up. I teach in the Religious Studies Program within the Center for Interdisciplinary Studies at Virginia Polytechnic Institute and State University in Blacksburg. Part of my teaching role in a public institution is to protect the religious freedom of each of my students as we explore together scholarly approaches to the New Testament.

Item 2: I am a scholar and a writer.

I have written especially on the Gospel of Mark, but also on biblical literary criticism more generally and early Christian art. Since I have been reading and writing about the relatively short Gospel of Mark for twenty-something years, people occasionally ask if I am a slow reader! On this, please recall my previous remark to new readers of Mark's Gospel: It's a great book!

Item 3: I identify myself with the Christian tradition—in the somewhat complex relationship I presupposed of you above.

I was raised Methodist, then United Methodist. I am now an active member of Christ Episcopal Church in Blacksburg, Virginia, where I serve as a lector, Lay Eucharistic Minister, and sometime Sunday school teacher. The chapters in this book, although growing out of my twenty years of reading, writing about, and teaching the Gospel of Mark, derive most directly from four lectures I gave to six local churches during an ecumenical Lenten study in the year 2000. (The names of the churches are given in the Acknowledgments.) I am grateful to the members of these churches who were my engaged and engaging audience—for my book, like Mark's, was written to be heard.

The following four chapters look at all of Mark's Gospel in narrative order, from 1:1 through 16:8, but each chapter also focuses on a theme that is strong in that section. The themes are overlapping and interconnecting. At the close, a brief section offers echoes of these interrelated themes as they are played out for Mark's audience—in the first century and in the twenty-first. Perhaps in the end we will have ears to hear the power of the beginning: "The beginning of the gospel of Jesus Christ, the Son of God."

Kingdom

Mark 1:1–4:34

O God,
that we like Jesus might be called
your sons and daughters,
give us ears to hear the Gospel of Mark
as good news of your kingdom
breaking into the world through our lives.
Amen.

The beginning of the gospel of Jesus Christ, the Son of God.
(Mark 1:1)

The first verse of this Gospel is particularly interesting because something's missing. If you were to turn in something like this opening to your English teacher—or a picky boss—you would get the comment: "incomplete sentence." On your computer screen you might see wavy green underlining. Mark 1:1 is missing a verb. Some people try to supply a verb by saying, "This is the beginning of the gospel of Jesus Christ, the Son of God." This effort seems misguided. When the president is giving a press conference the host doesn't say, "This is the president of the United States." Presumably everyone knows that. The host says—with a certain formality: "The president of the United States." It's a proclamation. And that's what Mark 1:1 is, a proclamation. In fact, it's serving as a title for the whole book. "The Gospel according to Mark" wasn't added until later. This is the way the book titles itself. So we should think carefully about each of the words in the title.

THE BEGINNING OF THE **GOSPEL** OF JESUS CHRIST, THE SON OF GOD.

We think, "Sure, the Gospel according to Mark." No, not quite. What we mean by Gospel is Matthew, Mark, Luke, or John—a religious story about the meaning of the life and death of Jesus. But that's not what Mark meant by *gospel;* it wasn't what Paul meant by *gospel.* They meant the "good news." The good news *of* Jesus probably meant the good news that he spoke, the good news that he proclaimed. In Greek the phrase can also be taken as the good news *about* Jesus, the good news about who he was. So "the beginning of the gospel" doesn't mean the beginning of the book. That would be like wearing a T-shirt that says "T-shirt." Of course it's the beginning of the book, but it's the title of the whole book.

In the Greco-Roman world the term *gospel* was used in imperial proclamations to refer to the "good news" of the emperor's appearance, ordinances, or military victories. Since politics and religion were not separated realms in the ancient world, Mark's proclamation of the "good news" *of Jesus* may challenge this imperial presumption.

THE BEGINNING OF THE GOSPEL OF **JESUS** CHRIST, THE SON OF GOD.

Jesus is the bottom line of the Gospel: without Jesus there would be no Gospels; but Jesus did not, of course, write the Gospels. Nor were the Gospel writers particularly interested in writing objective biographies of Jesus, although, since the early nineteenth century, some readers have wished (or assumed) they were. Mark's Gospel portrays Jesus not in the way of an ID photo (for a driver's license, for example) but in the manner of a painted portrait commissioned from a talented artist. The goal is not simply to identify Jesus—no plain background, blank stare, or red eyes here! The goal is to portray Jesus as the bearer of the "good news" of God's kingdom. The portrait is lovingly and dramatically painted to achieve that effect.

One could, of course, use the Gospels (along with other resources) as reference materials in a quest for the historical Jesus. Many scholars have been and are currently engaged in that complex and significant task. But this book is not. This guide to hearing Mark's Gospel is interested in how Jesus is portrayed as a character in this dramatic story. Often I will use the phrase "the Markan Jesus" to make this point of view explicit. But even when I simply write Jesus, it is the Markan Jesus that I mean.

THE BEGINNING OF THE GOSPEL OF JESUS **CHRIST**, THE SON OF GOD.

My students sometimes think that Christ is Jesus' last name—as if it would be alphabetized under the Cs—Christ, Jesus. Actually it's not a name at all; it's a title. Christ comes from the Greek *Christos,* which translates the Hebrew word *messiah.* Messiah/the Christ is the same word in different languages. Messiah means the one who is anointed, the anointed one. In ancient Israel instead of crowning the king, the officials would anoint him—with oil. It sounds awful, but it's not like pouring on cooking oil; it's more like smoothing on an ointment, like the chrism used in baptism in some churches. Anointing means that this person is set aside, marked out, sealed as special because of a special task that he or she has from God. So Jesus is one of these people who is called out by God for a special task.

THE BEGINNING OF THE GOSPEL OF JESUS CHRIST, THE **SON OF GOD**.

"Son of God" appears in 1:1 in some ancient manuscripts and not in others. Surely we know what that phrase means; it conveys Jesus' divinity, right? That's what the phrase means to many people today, but in the first-century Jewish and earliest Christian world it would have carried a different meaning. The concept of Jesus' divinity develops a little later in Christian tradition. "Son of God" would have meant someone who is obedient to God. It's interesting that in the ancient world the main concept of a son was someone who obeys the father. I have a wonderful son, but obedience is not his most striking trait. I accept this difference as one of those cultural gaps between the first century and the twenty-first. If a son is one who obeys the father, "Son of God" means a righteous person, one who obeys God. Sometimes the designation "son of God" was used for all of Israel: "out of Egypt I called my son" (Hosea 11:1). Sometimes it was applied to the king: "You are my son; today I have begotten you" (Psalm 2:7). And sometimes it was applied to any righteous individual: "for if the righteous man is God's child [son], he will help him" (Wisdom of Solomon 2:18).

THE **BEGINNING** OF THE GOSPEL OF JESUS CHRIST, THE SON OF GOD.

The final word of the title to consider is its first word, "beginning." That I think is the oddest word in the title. To call your whole story "the beginning of the good news of Jesus Christ, the Son of God" does seem strange. Some scholars think it's so strange that it must be just the title for the first part of the story, about John the Baptist. The problem with that theory is that this is the only section in the whole book with a heading! If you were going to make headings, you'd probably make more than one of them—unless you were making a title. It does seem to me that it's the title of the whole narrative. I ask you to think about it this way: Mark proclaims the beginning of the good news of Jesus Christ, the Son of God; what would the ending be? If there were an ending to this good news, then that would be very bad news indeed—the bad news that the kingdom of God is no longer breaking into history. According to Mark, this story is the beginning because the ending has not yet occurred. The culmination will not occur, of course, until the end time, when Jesus comes with power, but even that will not be the ending: "Heaven and earth will pass away, but my words will not pass away" (Mark 13:31 NRSV). The world may end, but the good news is always beginning.

Rest assured I'm not going to discuss all the verses of Mark in as much detail as I have discussed the title! Titles, as emblematic of their stories, deserve a little extra attention. For this listener's guide to Mark's Gospel I have divided the text into four major sections and given each a thematic title.

1:1–4:34	Kingdom
4:35–8:26	Community
8:22–10:52	Discipleship
11:1–16:8	Suffering

One could argue for other divisions. One could suggest other thematic titles. The process of thinking about how parts fit together and how emphases interrelate is more important than the product (outlines and labels) that may result. This is *a* listener's guide, not *the* (only, definitive) listener's guide. In that spirit I am going to further subdivide Mark 1:1–4:34 into four subsections: 1:1–45, Jesus and the kingdom of God; 2:1–3:6, Jesus and the traditional community; 3:7–35, Jesus and the new community; 4:1–34, Jesus and parables of the kingdom.

JESUS AND THE KINGDOM OF GOD (MARK 1:1–45)

Here we are, ready for "the beginning of the gospel of Jesus Christ, the Son of God," and we get not Jesus, but John.

John the Baptizer (Mark 1:2–8)

In fact, we get Mark, the Gospel writer, telling us that Isaiah said that someone will come in the wilderness preparing the way of the Lord. Then, just as promised, somebody shows up, and he's in the wilderness saying, "I'm preparing the way for someone after me." So when John appears in the wilderness, he fulfills the prophecy of Isaiah that was just quoted. He proclaims a baptism for repentance, which means turning around from evil ways and turning in a good direction. Then, although this is a very short section, we hear a bit about what John wears—camel's hair and a leather belt—and what he eats—locusts and wild honey. We are given this information because we are supposed to be aware of biblical stories about prophets; we are supposed to know—aha, he dresses like Elijah (2 Kings 1:8; compare Zechariah 13:4), he eats like Elijah, and we know that Elijah is coming before the end time (Malachi 4:5). Elijah is coming before the day of the Lord comes because he's available—he didn't die; he took the chariot up to heaven, so he's alive and available to come back before the final judgment. And then John says someone greater is coming. So by the time Jesus enters the scene we know who he is going to be, not because the title says Jesus is the Christ, but because here we get to prove it to ourselves by following the pointers. Mark points to Isaiah, and Isaiah points to John, and John points to Jesus, and Jesus is the one who comes, and he comes to be baptized also for repentance.

Jesus' Baptism (Mark 1:9–11)

Others are baptized by John as well, but only in the case of Jesus does the narrator present a response to the baptism on the part of God: the heavens split—it's a strong verb—they tear apart. The heavens are that which separates God from humanity, a kind of boundary line between God and humanity, and the boundary rips. Something about the beginning here means that the wall between God and humanity is shattered. Then the Spirit descends like a dove on Jesus—another indicator that the distance between God and humanity is being bridged. A voice from the heaven says, "You are my son." Now the title has signaled us to watch out for that: "the Son of God." The audience figures out, of course, that the voice from the heaven is God. And God says, "You are my son." So the audience thinks, "Wow, what is the voice going to ask Jesus to do? We haven't quite figured out what his special task from God is yet, but Jesus is going to be the Messiah; he is going to be the Son of God. That ought to be a cushy life."

Jesus' Testing (Mark 1:12–13)

And the next thing we know, the Spirit, which had just descended on him, "throws him out" into the wilderness! Translations usually say "drove him out" (NRSV), and that's pretty good. It's certainly not "led him out." It's "throws." A few verses later on Jesus is going to "throw" unclean spirits out of people, and here the most clean spirit throws Jesus out. So, yes, being the Messiah could be good, but it's not going to be easy.

Jesus is in the wilderness, where people don't ordinarily live, for forty days. Mark's audience, steeped in biblical narratives, is thinking—forty in the wilderness, forty in the wilderness. We remember the exodus story and the forty years of testing the people of Israel experienced in the wilderness. And did they all pass the test? No, they did not. Does Jesus pass the test? A+. He more than passes the test, and how do we know? Because he is "with the wild beasts"—peacefully; he is with the wild beasts—and they don't eat him up! Rather, angels, that is, messengers of God, minister to him; they serve him. The Greek verb used here, *diakoneō*, is later used in its noun form for "deacons." So the angels might be said to serve as deacons to Jesus. Thus it's clear that he has passed the test, and he's passed the test against Satan. Satan is in charge of the forces of evil, and Jesus is clearly aligned with God and the forces of good.

Reviewing Mark 1:2–13—Jesus and God

Thus, we have three scenes in rapid succession: John, Jesus' baptism, and Jesus' testing. In each case the audience asks, Who is Jesus in relation to God? The answer is the Messiah, the Christ, the one anointed by God for a special task. And, as Son of God, he is going to be obedient to God in that task. But we're still not clear what the task is. We have to keep listening to gain that clarity.

Jesus' Preaching (Mark 1:14–15)

We hear that, after John was arrested . . . Did we miss that part? Do you remember reading about John's arrest? Well, we haven't read about it yet, but it is assumed that we know other stories besides the ones told here. There would still have been stories circulating in the oral tradition when the Gospel was reduced to writing. What happens after John was arrested is the shortest sermon that was ever preached and perhaps the most powerful. It's a three-line sermon Jesus preaches in Galilee: "The time is fulfilled, and the kingdom of God has come near; repent and believe in the good news" (NRSV).

The word for time is especially interesting. There are two Greek words for time: *chronos*, which means—you know, 7:30 p.m., 8:30 p.m., 9:30 p.m., all in chronological order; and *kairos*, which refers to the quality of time, a special quality of time—like when you say, "It's taking forever for my best friend to get here!" In Jesus' day and in Mark's day, many people had the feeling that they were coming to the end of the age. It looked as if God was *not* in charge of the world because all these evil forces had taken over, but very soon God would come back in a dramatic way. For the Markan Jesus, the *kairos* has come. It's now; it's happening now. It's not completely fulfilled yet, but it's breaking into history—God's kingdom or empire, God's rulership or reign. Kingdom is not a place; kingdom is an activity of God as ruler. God is coming near as ruler now, believe it or not, and it's a gift. So what we should do in response is repent: turn around, get facing God, and believe—or better, trust—trust in goodness, trust in God's goodness.

First Disciples (Mark 1:16–20)

Then immediately it's as if Jesus says, "Wow, this is a huge job—proclaiming the kingdom of God. I can't do this by myself. This is not a one-man job. This is something for which we need to have community. We need a whole group of people working together." So the first thing Jesus does is go out and get some followers. He goes by the Sea of Galilee and calls Simon and Andrew, two brothers. (Simon will later receive the nickname Peter.) And he says, "You want to fish? Come and fish for people." Interesting metaphor—fishing for people. Did you ever stop to think: Do fish like to be caught? Do people like to be caught? This metaphor comes from apocalyptic Judaism, Judaism that focuses on the end time. At the end time there will be a judgment, and the fish will be caught in the net and will all be sorted out. So somehow these followers are going to help in that gathering activity that anticipates the coming judgment.

Immediately Simon and Andrew leave their work; they leave their nets and follow Jesus. One thing we notice is that there must be more to the story than this. John was arrested, Jesus gives a three-line sermon, he calls Simon and Andrew, and they immediately follow him. Amazing! But this is a synopsis. Immediately they follow him. Then he sees two more fishermen, James and John, and he calls them. Their father is with them, their family. What do you do with your family? This kind of proclamation is going to require people to leave behind some conventional roles. Maybe our work and our family are going to have different degrees of importance than they used to before we were followers of Jesus.

Teaching and Casting Out a Demon (Mark 1:21–28)

Jesus moves on into Capernaum. It's the Sabbath, and Jesus, being Jewish (as are most of the characters in Mark's story), goes to the synagogue. There he teaches (as any adult male could), but he teaches as one who has authority and not as the scribes. Now the scribes have their authority, which is derived authority; it comes from being interpreters of the Scripture, of the things that are written. Jesus' authority seems different; it seems to be coming almost from himself, or even directly from God, and not through a process of learning. But before we can meditate on that feature too long there appears in the synagogue a man with an unclean spirit. And the unclean spirit, who could talk, of course, talks to Jesus and recognizes Jesus as "the Holy One of God." We realize—aha, we heard a phrase like that before, "the Son of God." So the unclean spirit recognizes who Jesus is in relation to God.

Interestingly, the spirit world—the evil spirit world and the good spirit world—communicates in a way not open to ordinary humans. We can imagine a world of the spirit, including the Holy Spirit and God, in which Jesus participates, and an opposing world of Satan, demons, and unclean spirits. The two worlds communicate with each other in ways that ordinary humans do not comprehend. In this episode Satan's side already knows it's going to lose; it's losing ground. The unclean spirit sees Jesus for the first time and says, "I know who you are. I've heard that such a person is coming to overturn the forces of evil."

The people's response is interesting. They've just seen Jesus throw out this demon, and they say, "What is this, a new teaching with authority?" They might be expected to say, "What is this, a new type of exorcising with authority?" We have the teaching, then there's the exorcism, and then they say, "What a remarkable teaching!" The narrator also says, "He commands even the unclean spirits, and they obey him" (NRSV). But the story tells us that the teaching and the exorcising are somehow connected. We might pull them apart because we think we can understand the teaching better than we can the exorcising. We have different ways of explaining illness than unclean spirits. We talk about unclean germs, which would have been just as invisible in the first century as unclean spirits are to most people in the twenty-first. But here the teaching and the exorcising are very much together; we have a sort of sandwich: a reference to teaching (A), a reference to exorcising (B), a reference to teaching (A). And what do teaching and exorcising have in common? They both show Jesus' power. The kingdom of God is breaking in. How could Satan's kingdom be under attack unless God's kingdom was on the move?

Healing a Fever (Mark 1:29–31)

After they leave the synagogue they go to a house, to Simon's house apparently; at least Simon's mother-in-law is there. Normally she would serve them, but she can't; she's in bed with a fever. Jesus heals her fever just like that, and she ministers to them. Does that sound familiar? She serves them; she "deacons" them. The word is only used a few times in Mark's Gospel, and two of the times are here: angels minister to Jesus at his testing in the wilderness, and Simon's mother-in-law serves him in this way as well. In addition, there are two healing stories here that may be heard in concert: a man is healed in the synagogue, a public place, the place of men in Jesus' culture; a woman is healed in a home, the place of women. The audience must at least conclude that Jesus doesn't play favorites. Both men and women are healed. Gender is not a barrier. Social location is not a barrier. Mark can't tell about *everyone* Jesus healed, so he's showing us a sample and assuming that we will draw an appropriate conclusion.

Healing Many (Mark 1:32–34)

In case we don't, he gives us a summary statement in verses 33–34, saying that many sick are cured. People are coming from all over, and many demons are cast out. Jesus will not let the demons speak because they know him. This is a very strange thing. Scholars call it the "messianic secret." Jesus is the Christ, the Messiah, but he's always saying, "Don't tell; don't tell; it's a secret." Some of my students have pointed out, "Yeah, if I were Jesus I wouldn't want the demons doing my P.R. for me either." The students have a point: If you're on the side of God, you don't want the demons spreading the story about you.

But even if the human beings said everything they knew about Jesus so far, what would they say? "He gives short sermons. That's good. Powerful sermons. He heals people." So he's a powerful healer and powerful teacher. There were a number of those running around in the ancient world, more healers than we hear about today, and more preachers. So healing and preaching—that's okay, but that isn't particularly distinctive. And is that the whole story? Mrs. Jones, my ninth-grade English teacher, had a sign on the class bulletin board: "Beware of the half-truth. You may have hold of the wrong half." For Mark it is clearly the wrong half if you tell about Jesus as a powerful healer and preacher. So if you haven't heard the whole story yet, wait, wait.

Praying and Preaching (Mark 1:35–39)

Then Jesus goes out to the wilderness (NRSV: "a deserted place") to pray, to communicate with God. He's retreating; he's worn himself out with teaching and healing all the time. Simon goes looking for him and "tracks him down." That's a good translation, "tracks him down." It's not just looking for him; it's really what an animal does, like a dog hunts a deer. Simon and Andrew want to bring Jesus back because all these people are there waiting to be healed, and Jesus' first followers need some help. Jesus says, "Okay, okay. I'll go with you, but I'm not going back to *that* town; I'm going to the *next* town because that is why I came out." There's some urgency here. "I've got to keep moving because the end is coming and coming soon, and I really need to do what I set out to do, which is go out to lots of towns."

Healing a Leper (Mark 1:40–45)

A leper comes to Jesus and begs for healing, or cleansing. You probably know that leprosy can refer to a number of skin diseases in the ancient world, but it always means a type of disease that socially isolates the victim. The ancients did know that some forms of the disease were very contagious, so sufferers were isolated. Jesus is moved with pity for the man and heals him. And Jesus says, "Don't tell anybody." That's going to be just a little bit impossible. But he adds, "Don't tell anybody; go tell this body." So obviously Jesus doesn't mean literally "don't tell anybody"; he means, "Don't brag about this; don't spread this word widely, but do go to the priest and make the appropriate sacrifice in thanksgiving to God for your cleansing and obtain the certificate of wholeness/holiness. Work within the system; work within the system and give your thanks to God." So the audience realizes that Jesus is attributing his power to heal directly to God. Now Jesus' fame spreads so much that he can't even go into a town any more. Wherever he goes, people come out to him.

Reviewing Mark 1:1–45—Jesus and the Kingdom of God

Thus three initial stories about how Jesus relates to God (John, Jesus' baptism, Jesus' testing) are followed by several stories about Jesus and the kingdom of God. Jesus preaches and calls disciples; he teaches and exorcises together, heals a fever and many sick people, preaches throughout Galilee and in the synagogue, and heals a leper. He seems to be making a big splash. Jesus knows that kingdom requires community, and the community seems to be responsive to his proclamation of the kingdom, the in-breaking reign of God.

JESUS AND THE TRADITIONAL COMMUNITY (MARK 2:1–3:6)

Then we move into a group of stories about Jesus and the traditional community.

Healing a Paralytic (Mark 2:1–12)

Jesus returns to Capernaum after some days; Capernaum is serving as his home base. Amid the crowd some friends lower a paralytic through the roof. They can't get to Jesus because the house is too crowded. So they dig through the roof—of a Palestinian mud wattle house, whose roof would be replaced every year after the rainy season anyway—and lower him down. Jesus is impressed. Jesus heals the paralyzed man, using the expression "Your sins are forgiven." It sounds like another healing story, but that last line is odd: "Your sins are forgiven."

Some scribes also hear that last line. These scribes have come down from Jerusalem—presumably to investigate Jesus—and they find that line odd indeed, so they ask, "Who are you to be forgiving sins?" Although, if you think about it, Jesus didn't say, "I forgive your sins"; he said, "Your sins are forgiven"; that's passive voice, probably meaning "Your sins are forgiven—by God. I just happen to know it because God and I are close." But the scribes say, "This is blasphemy." Jesus responds, "Not really; it's a sign that God has come near," but he adds, "The Son of Man has authority on earth to forgive sins."

The phrase "the Son of Man" is strange. Only Jesus uses it in Mark. It's probably a reference to the humanlike heavenly judge that is coming in the end time according to the book of Daniel (7:13–14), so it's an apocalyptic figure, someone at the end time. But when does Jesus think the end time is? Now! Or very close to now. It's beginning to happen right now. Another possibility is that the meaning of "son of man" in Aramaic, the spoken language of Jesus and his contemporaries, is behind the Greek here. In Aramaic, "son of man" is a reference to one's self. So we're not quite sure what it means, but we have room behind the healing story to have an ideological or theological fight.

Calling Levi and Eating with Sinners (Mark 2:13–17)

But we go on to the next story. Jesus teaches beside the sea, where he sees Levi, a tax collector, and he calls him. Even if you didn't know that most of the characters are Jewish, you might know that Levi is Jewish since "Levi" is the name of one of the twelve sons of Jacob, whose names are given to the twelve tribes of Israel. He's Jewish, but for whom is he collecting taxes or tolls? The Romans! So he's not going to be popular. Tax collectors aren't popular even when Romans are collecting taxes from Romans, but a Jew collecting Roman taxes from Jews is definitely unpopular—possibly even considered a sinner. Yet Jesus calls him to "Follow me," and Levi says, "All right, I will follow you," and he leaves his tax booth and follows him. Does that sound familiar? Jesus calls him. He leaves his work and follows him—just like the fishermen did. Afterwards Jesus goes to celebrate at a dinner with Levi. And there are other tax collectors there, and sinners, and the disciples.

So far this sounds like another call story, but the plot thickens when some say, "Ah, look, what is he doing with those people? He's eating with those people who are sinners; they're not clean people. We don't eat with unclean people." Jesus says, "I do. That's why I've come here. I've come not to call the righteous, but sinners. And if I'm going to make any headway with sinners, well, I need to have dinner with them, and I need to talk with them. What's happening here is the breaking-in of the kingdom of God. And the kingdom of God turns things topsyturvy; the righteous and the sinners sit at the same table; and the rich and the poor change places; the ins and the outs change places. That's what you're seeing. Can't you people hear this news as good?"

Question about Fasting (Mark 2:18–22)

Next we have a story about fasting. John's disciples are fasting. Did you know that John had disciples? Apparently so. And the disciples of the Pharisees are fasting, but Jesus' disciples are not. So some people ask Jesus why his disciples are not fasting, but he doesn't give them a straight answer. He says, "Ah, let me tell you poetically. You don't fast at the wedding party when the bridegroom is still there. You don't sew new cloth on old clothes. You don't put new wine in old wineskins." What do these images suggest? It's not too hard to figure out because there's a hint: "There will come a day when the bridegroom is taken away, and in that day there will be fasting." Who's the bridegroom? Jesus. When will he be taken way? At his death. So there will come a time for fasting, but not now. Now is the time for the party. (We'll come back again later to the phrase about the new wineskins and the new cloth.)

Plucking Grain on the Sabbath (Mark 2:23–28)

There follows a story about plucking grain on the Sabbath. At issue is whether this plucking grain, a minimal form of harvesting, is work and thus not permitted on the Sabbath. Presumably they're eating the grain—rubbing the heads together in their hands to remove the husks, then eating the kernels. Why else would they be plucking it? But the eating is not made explicit. What is explicit is a question to Jesus about his disciples' behavior. Jesus' response is surprising. He's in trouble with some members of his community already. Yet he says, "Well, if breaking the religious convention was good enough for David and his men, it's good enough for me and my followers. If it was good enough for the greatest king of the Jews, it's good enough for me, a country bumpkin from Galilee." Such a reply is hardly the way to win friends and influence Pharisees. Then Jesus adds, "The Sabbath was made for humankind, not humankind for the Sabbath; so the Son of Man is lord even of the Sabbath." Something of the future time is impinging on earth right now. The rules to honor God are also meant to honor human beings. Human beings should not have to be hungry on the Sabbath; that's not what God wants, and God has come near.

Healing a Withered Hand (Mark 3:1–6)

In the next story the religious authorities are waiting for Jesus in a synagogue on the Sabbath when a man with a withered hand appears. It looks like a setup. Jesus asks, "Is it lawful to do good or harm on the Sabbath? To save life or to kill?" You don't have to be a Pharisee to realize this question is not fair. I mean, one could easily ask, "Is it necessary to heal this man today, or could you wait one more day to heal him? How much harm would it do to wait one more day?" But Jesus says, "No, no. Is it lawful to do good or to do harm on the Sabbath?" He speaks with urgency: it's got to happen now; it's got to happen now; nothing can wait. Jesus asks the man to stretch out his hand, which is not actually a form of work. Jesus doesn't work; he just observes that when the hand is stretched out it is healed. The Pharisees and the Herodians, though, immediately conspire against him, how to destroy him. We're at chapter three in a book of sixteen chapters, and we already know this guy is going to get it. If we didn't catch it earlier with the bridegroom's being taken away, or with the Spirit's throwing him out into the wilderness, surely we catch it now.

Reviewing Mark 2:1–3:6—Jesus and the Traditional Community

So each of the five stories in this series (2:1–3:6), which look like healing stories and call narratives and things like that, ends in controversy. In addition, the stories are symmetrical.

2:1–12	healing a paralytic	(useless legs)
2:13–17	calling Levi/eating with sinners	(eating)
2:18–22	not fasting	(eating)
2:23–28	plucking grain on the Sabbath	(eating)
3:1–6	healing on the Sabbath	(useless hand)

In the beginning we have the healing of useless legs; in the end, the healing of a useless hand. In the middle we have things that have to do with eating. The disciples can't seem to get it right; they eat with the wrong people; they eat when they're supposed to be fasting; they eat on the wrong day. Nothing is quite right. These five stories in a row tell us that the beginning that looked so peaceful—with the traditional community, Jesus' own community, accepting his proclamation with amazement—soon became more problematic. And right in the center of this set of controversy stories is the saying about the wine and the cloth, the saying about the new and the old. Right in the center of all this controversy is the crucial question: How does the new relate to the old?

JESUS AND THE NEW COMMUNITY (MARK 3:7–35)

Yet we must have community. So if the old community, the traditional community, is not going to be as receptive as Jesus had first thought, then we're going to have to have a new community that will respond positively.

Healing Many (Mark 3:7–12)

In 3:7–12, we get a glimpse of how this new community is going to work. Here we have another summary statement. Every now and then Mark seems to say, "Wow, there's just so much stuff; I can't tell you everything, so I'll give you a little summary just to let you know I had to make choices." Jesus is again by the sea, the Sea of Galilee, and great multitudes from all over follow him. The listing of names of all the places the people come from is worth noting because Jesus is eventually going to go to most of those places. Before the word goes out from Jesus to all those places, all those places come symbolically to Jesus. Scholars have also pointed out that the places mentioned are the furthest boundaries of King David's kingdom. King David was the greatest king of Israel and had the largest kingdom. All of Israel, Israel to its fullest extent, seems to be coming to hear Jesus.

And Jesus heals many. And unclean spirits say, "You are the Son of God." It's almost as if the unclean spirits had read the title of the Gospel with its reference to "Jesus Christ, the Son of God." But, of course, it's the audience who has heard the title. Good titles work on hearers and readers. Good titles make some sense in the beginning, but their full significance dawns on us as we move through the story. When we get to the last chapter, the last page, then we really understand the title. That happens with good titles, and Mark's is a good one. In response to the knowing unclean spirits, Jesus says, "Do not make me known." The messianic secret is still on. "Don't go telling everybody; don't go telling anybody. You've got to hear the whole story before you have enough to tell."

Naming Twelve (Mark 3:13–19a)

Then Jesus appoints twelve. The narrator says that Jesus went up on the mountain. Now you don't want to get too literal about that mountain. Six verses ago Jesus and his followers were by the sea. I've seen places on the Mediterranean where the mountains go down to the sea, but the mountains don't go down to the sea on the west side of the Sea of Galilee. So the mountain is probably more theological than geographical. A mountain symbolizes communication between God—up in the usual view—and humans, who are on the earth. A mountain is as close as humans can get to God and where God can most easily get down to earth. It's a place where humans and God communicate, like Moses communicates with God on a mountain. On the mountain Jesus names twelve. He's got a lot of followers; he's called some and healed others, but, even though many follow him, Jesus designates twelve particularly. Now we know that twelve is a very special number in this connection because of the twelve tribes of Israel. The people of God were organized into twelve tribes. We've just gone through a series of stories that suggests that the leaders of Israel are not necessarily going to be the leaders of the new community. We've had some friction there. But we're still going to need community leaders, so here's a new twelve. There's going to be a new Israel, so we have a new twelve.

Notice what the twelve are assigned to do. They have to do two things, and the second thing also has two parts. They are to be with Jesus and to be sent out. These are the two motions of discipleship: to be with him—and to be with each other in community—and soon after that to have enough energy to be sent out. Now when they are sent out they do two things: they preach, or proclaim the message, and they cast out demons. That's what Jesus has been doing recently—preaching and casting out demons. So that's what the twelve do; they have to be with him so they can learn the basics of what he's doing. That's the way it is between a master and his disciples; they learn from doing.

The names of the twelve are given. We even get some nicknames. We find out that Simon is called Peter, which means "rock." It turns out there's a bit of irony there because Peter is sometimes more like a jellyfish than a rock. We find out that James and John, sons of Zebedee, are called "Sons of Thunder." It makes you want to meet Zebedee, doesn't it! And we find out that the last person named is "Judas Iscariot, who betrayed him." So much for suspense. The listing of the twelve is their big scene; they come out and take a bow, and Judas is introduced as the betrayer. This is not a book that promises a surprise ending. There are indeed surprises in the ending, but, since we saw the Spirit throw Jesus out into the wilderness early on, and we heard the Pharisees and the Herodians plotting against him not much later, knowing now that Judas Iscariot is going to betray him at the end is not a complete shock. Ancient audiences frequently knew the endings of their stories in the beginning. The attraction was to see just how one got there. In Mark's story, we know what's coming, but Mark thinks it's going to take us some time to get ready for it. It's best to heed his warnings.

Jesus' Family (Mark 3:19b–21)

Next we have a story about Jesus' family. Jesus goes to his home, and the crowd is there. The crowd is always there. And the family comes, perhaps to rescue him because people are saying, "He's crazy; he's really out of his mind; he's saying these weird things about the kingdom of God coming near." Does the family think he's crazy? The narrator doesn't say that. He says the family heard that other people were saying he's crazy. So they come to get him, and . . . the story line is left hanging.

Jesus and Some Scribes (Mark 3:22–30)

Meanwhile some scribes who had come from Jerusalem say, "Oh, we know why he's crazy; he's crazy like a fox. He can cast out these demons because he's on the side of the demons. He's working a kind of evil magic; clearly he's not on the side of good because we're on the side of good. We represent God; we're on the side of good. Since he's not on our side, he must be on the other side; he must be on Satan's side." Jesus responds, "You're not using good judgment. Think about it.   The unclean spirits that I'm casting out are connected to Satan, and Satan would not be casting out Satan. I'm winning *against* Satan. So I can't be on that side." And Jesus adds, "A house divided against itself cannot stand." When I was saying this in the classroom once, a student interjected, "Abraham Lincoln said that." I responded, "That's true, but Abraham Lincoln got it from Jesus." A house divided cannot stand; a kingdom divided cannot stand. The kingdom Jesus proclaims, God's kingdom, is not divided and falling. Satan's kingdom is falling, not because it is divided against itself (with Jesus casting out demons from within Satan's domain), but because Satan (as the strong man) has been tied up and his house is being plundered as part of the in-breaking kingdom of God.

The Holy Spirit has empowered Jesus to proclaim the reign of God. Thus, confusing the work of God with the work of Satan is blasphemy against the Holy Spirit. The "unforgivable sin" is not some failure to uphold conventional morality; it is the willful attempt to view good as evil—or evil as good.

Jesus' Metaphorical Family (Mark 3:31–35)

Then the family is back; actually they've stayed there all along, waiting. So many people are in the house they can't get in, so they send a message, "Your mother and brothers and sisters are outside asking for you." And Jesus responds, "Who are my mother and brothers and sisters?" He looks around at those people crowding into the house with him, and he says, "Whoever does the will of God is my brother and sister and mother."   Some scholars think, "Aha, Jesus rejected his family." That could be, but you don't learn it from here. Maybe Jesus did walk away from his family like James and John walked away from their father in the boat. But I think what's happening here is that Mark's Jesus is saying, "I'm a teacher, and I can't resist the possibility of a metaphor for instructing you about the new community of the kingdom." Jesus moves from one level to another.

We do know that in the first century the family was a crucial institution that was often split by persons who came to the conviction that Jesus was the Christ. In the Jewish community, those who believed in Jesus as the Christ were definitely a minority. If your family was Jewish, your following Christ might cause division. If you were in a pagan family, the belief in just one God would have seemed kind of weird. How could one God handle everything? As a believer in the Christ, you might be judged "crazy" and cut off from part of your family. And what would you call your new family in Christ? Brothers and sisters. (Read Paul's letters: "brothers and sisters.") So we do know that in early Christianity the congregation became a family for people in a real way. Did Jesus reject his biological family? We cannot tell from this text. What we can hear and tell is that the "new community" understands itself as a family of "whoever does the will of God."

Reviewing Mark 1–3

Mark 1:1–45   Jesus and the Kingdom of God
Mark 2:1–3:6   Jesus and the Traditional Community
Mark 3:7–35   Jesus and the New Community

As Mark's audience, we began by looking at Jesus in relation to God (in terms of the title, in terms of John the Baptist and his baptism of Jesus, in terms of Jesus' testing) and in relation to the reign of God (including his powerful teaching and powerful healing). At first it seemed the response to Jesus' proclamation was going to be positive and unproblematic. But then we heard five controversy stories that suggested it wasn't going to be all that easy. It was going to be more complicated; some toes were being stepped on. Like Jesus, most of his followers are Jewish. Where he gets into trouble is with the Jewish authorities, the Jewish leaders. (Sometimes twenty-first-century Christian readers do not realize—or remember—that Mark's Gospel portrays conflict *within* a religious community, the diverse first-century Jewish community, not between two religious traditions, "Judaism" and "Christianity.") So Jesus establishes a new community not only with "the twelve," symbolic of the twelve tribes of Israel, but also with a broader group of "whoever does the will of God."

JESUS AND PARABLES OF THE KINGDOM (MARK 4:1–34)

With that foundation, we move to chapter 4, which presents parables of the kingdom of God. It's as if the Markan Jesus thinks, "Okay, now that I've got the new community established, with the twelve and whoever does the will of God, I'm going to explain what the kingdom of God is like and what one can expect as part of God's reign." The word *parable* comes from two Greek words that mean "to throw along side of." Basically a parable throws two things side by side, forming a comparison. Usually it throws together an image from the concrete world, the ordinary, everyday life world, with something that's abstract. A parable helps to make clear an abstract thing that's hard to get a handle on; what is difficult to grasp is explained in terms of something concrete that is more easily understood. We can tell from the things that Jesus chooses to make parables out of that his is an agricultural culture. People who plant seeds are the target audience for these powerful little stories.

Parable of the Seeds (Mark 4:1–9)

The narrator makes a point to locate Jesus in relation to the sea: the people are on the land by the sea, and Jesus gets into the boat on the sea. In addition, after Jesus is in the boat on the sea talking to the people on the land, he talks about seeds that are planted in the land. The Greek word *ge* signifies both "land" and "earth." A smooth English translation requires two different words, but in Mark's Greek text the word repetition is quite noticeable. Jesus is on the sea talking about the land.

What Jesus says is that the sower sows the seed, and it looks like it's not going to make a productive crop because he sows it everywhere. Some seed falls on the path, where it doesn't grow very well; and some falls on rocky soil, where it gets a good start and then withers. Some falls on thorns, and the thorns win; and just a little bit falls on good earth. So what do we expect? A mediocre harvest? But what we get is a fantastic harvest. Thirtyfold, sixtyfold, a hundredfold! About eightfold would be a normal harvest. So a hundredfold is ridiculous; this is a stretch. This is hyperbole. This is not a farmer's almanac but a parable of the kingdom of God. The reign of God is like that; you look around and you see . . . a carpenter from Nazareth telling stories. That's really promising, God. But what has started small is going to get big. That's the parable's impact. A refrain keeps coming into this chapter: Let anyone with ears to hear, listen. Look around, who has ears? That's probably everybody. But ears to hear? There's something in the parable you have to puzzle over. "Parable" can also be translated "riddle." It's something like a riddle that teases you into thought.

Parables and Mystery (Mark 4:10–12)

The next few verses seem to offer an explanation for Jesus' speaking in parables. If you have a study Bible with subheadings, it probably says, "the reason for speaking in parables" or "the purpose of the parables." "Oh, good," you think, "now I'll understand." But it doesn't really help much. Notice first that when Jesus was alone, those who were with him along with the twelve asked him concerning the parables. That's a strange way to be alone—alone with twelve people plus other people! It just means Jesus wasn't with the crowd. When he wasn't with the crowd, his followers asked him to explain the parables. And Jesus says, "Well, to you, my in-group, has been given the mystery of the kingdom of God. But to those outside, everything happens in parables." "Everything happens in parables"—very strange phrase, in Greek and in English. "To you has been given the mystery"—if you check the NRSV, you'll see it says "secret." In fact, the footnote says "mystery." I think "mystery" is a better translation; the Greek word is *mysterion.* When you say someone has given you the secret, you feel like, "I have the answer. I can open the door; I have the key." But it's not really like that here. Being given the *mystery* of the kingdom of God seems less like getting the answer and more like getting the question, which is usually more important anyway. But, in any case, there's a separation between the disciples, who receive the mystery from someone else (the passive voice suggests God), and everyone else, for whom everything happens in parables. Things keep happening in riddles, and many don't understand.

Next comes an allusion to Isaiah. The author of Mark assumes the audience is familiar with the biblical tradition and recognizes allusions. (Matthew doesn't seem to trust his audience quite so much, so he states that Isaiah is being quoted at this point, just in case the listeners don't pick it up. See Matthew 13:10–17.) The allusion is to Isaiah 6. In this chapter, Isaiah remembers what it was like to be called as God's prophet. The drift of his thought is this: "God, you knew in the beginning that you were going to send me out to preach to people, and they were going to hear, and they weren't going to understand. They were going to see, but they weren't going to understand. And you knew that from the beginning, and you still sent me out there to do it! And I did it. And you were right; they didn't understand." Remembering this Isaiah passage helped lessen the frustration of a person sent out by God for a special task when a positive reception was lacking. It was an important story for early Christians. Not only does it occur in Mark, it occurs in Matthew, Luke, John, and Acts. It's that important. The experience of being unheard happened over and over again—to Jesus, to Paul, to Mark. Remembering Isaiah's frustration offered consolation: "We're not the first ones to whom this has happened, you know. It happened to Isaiah. God didn't say, 'I anointed you to be a prophet (or messiah or a preacher) everyone's going to understand. I didn't anoint understanding in everyone.'"

Interpreting the Parable of the Seeds (Mark 4:13–20)

Then we come to an interpretation of the parable of the seeds (or, more traditionally, the parable of the sower). Actually, it's more of an allegory. The difference between an allegory and a parable is that an allegory lines things up. The sower is the one who sows the seed; the seed is the word; and this is that, and that is this. The birds that come to eat the seed off the path represent Satan. Could you have puzzled that out? That the birds represent Satan? You must know the key to the allegory. Most scholars think this allegorical interpretation was developed later than the time of Jesus. In some ways allegory operates against parable—closing off thought rather than opening it up, giving the answer rather than a question.

See What You Hear (Mark 4:21–25)

The whole point of telling the parable is that somehow it's going to make sense. So nothing's hidden that won't be exposed; no one lights a lamp and puts it under a bushel. However, you've got to have the right kind of ears, and you've got to have the right kind of eyes. It's not spoon-feeding. Some interpretation of the parable is required—a dialogue among the people who are listening. There's a wonderful phrase presented here. In the NRSV it reads, "Pay attention to what you hear." That's pretty lame. But in the Greek it's more like, "See what you hear"; "Watch what you see"; "Look out for what you hear." When language is used in that way, against itself, it presents another dimension. We can't be too literal here, folks. In addition to merging one sense (hearing) into another (seeing), we've got "Those who receive, those who have something already, will receive more, and those who don't have anything now will lose that." That's illogical. I don't have anything at all, and I'm going to lose the nothing at all that I don't have? Clearly we're at the language-breaking metaphor stage. We're supposed to be thinking beyond the literal level.

Parable of the Seed Growing of Itself (Mark 4:26–29)

Then we have the little story of the seed growing of itself. The kingdom of God is as if . . . This is the parable, the throwing together. A sower sows the seed, then he sleeps, then he wakes, and sleeps and wakes. The seed grows, and he didn't make it grow; he just put it there. It grows of itself, which means God provides the growth. Guess what? That's why they call it the kingdom *of God*, because God brings it, because God makes it happen. It's not the kingdom of Jesus. It's not the kingdom of Peter and Paul or somebody else. It's the kingdom of God. Jesus proclaims it: "Look what God is doing! Look what God is doing!" Jesus doesn't make it happen. He points out that it is happening. He announces it, but it is the kingdom of God. Jesus sleeps and wakes just like the sower, and the kingdom comes. Then the Markan Jesus mentions the harvest, a typical image in apocalyptic Judaism. Harvesting grain, like sorting the fish in the net, refers to the end time. And the seed is already planted. And the seed is already growing. So the harvest cannot be that far away.

Parable of the Mustard Seed (Mark 4:30–32)

Then we have the famous parable of the mustard seed. Did you ever have a necklace with a mustard seed in it? I can't find mine—it's such a tiny seed, you know. The parable is a lovely story: a tiny seed, the tiniest of all seeds in the earth, Mark tells us, is planted and grows into this incredibly big—uh—shrub. It's a great big bush. Now you can imagine a more melodramatic story that goes something like, "A little cedar seed was planted, and it became a majestic cedar of Lebanon." Or a tiny redwood seed became a giant redwood. Or an acorn became a spreading oak tree. However, both Ezekiel 31 and Daniel 4 narrate stories of mighty trees—allegories for great but ungodly nations—that are cut down! The Markan Jesus says, "Well, you know, God's kingdom is really more like a lowly mustard bush." And you're thinking, "Is that good?

We don't need a lot of mustard bushes. Mustard is sort of like a weed. If you plant one, you'll wish you hadn't because then you'll have more." I think if I were translating the parable into our day I would say, "The kingdom of God is like a person who plants a dandelion seed." Does anyone plant a dandelion? If you plant one, they just keep coming. The kingdom of God—is it under your control? Does it pop up where you want it to pop up? It just pops up wherever; it just keeps coming and coming. The kingdom of God is like that. The rule of God is something that spreads very quietly—but very insistently. Ever try to get rid of dandelions? There's just no way. And the kingdom of God is like that.

Hearing the Parables (Mark 4:33–34)

At the end of the parable section we come to this statement, "With many such parables, he spoke the word to them, as they were able to hear it; he did not speak to them except in parables, but he explained everything in private to his disciples" (4:34 NRSV). So, would that make his disciples insiders and the crowd outsiders? Or, if this is connected with the controversies with the Jewish leaders, maybe the disciples and the crowd together are insiders and the Jewish leaders are outsiders? Or, maybe the Jewish audience understands the Jews to be insiders and the Gentiles to be outsiders? We can't really tell. Besides, what does it mean to be an insider? Is it easy? Is it really obvious what you gain when you're an insider? Does being an insider free you from having to ponder the parables of the kingdom of God? Does being an insider free you from having to have ears to hear? Does it tone down the surprising nature of the kingdom? These are excellent questions to ask as we move on to the next section of Mark's Gospel. What does it mean to be an insider? Who's an insider? Who's an outsider? What difference does it make? What does the coming of the kingdom of God change?

> *O God,*
> *that we like Jesus might be called*
> *your sons and daughters,*
> *give us ears to hear the Gospel of Mark*
> *as good news of your kingdom*
> *breaking into the world through our lives.*
> *Amen.*

Community

Mark 4:35–8:26

O God,
that we, like Jesus, might be brothers and sisters
with all your people,
give us ears to hear the Gospel of Mark
as good news for an inclusive community
beyond the boundaries that restrict our love.
Amen.

We're looking at Mark's Gospel in four sections, and the current section is the second one, 4:35–8:26, and the topic is community. I talked a lot about community in relation to the first section, Mark 1:1–4:34, where the focus was the kingdom and Jesus being the proclaimer of the kingdom of God breaking into history. The first thing Jesus does after his three-line sermon that initiates that proclamation is to go call disciples because one needs a community. Now we're going to consider the boundaries of that community. The Markan Jesus pushes the boundaries of that community, the community gathered in anticipation of the coming of the kingdom of God.

It's difficult to divide chapters 4 through 8 into smaller subsections. Themes and types of events repeat themselves in various locales. There are healings, there are teachings; the disciples do some of the teaching and healing as well. There are "mighty deeds" and journeys. Events happen on the Sea of Galilee; there are travels back and forth across the Sea of Galilee. The section is loosely organized as a trip or tour. Sometimes Jesus is with Jews, sometimes with Gentiles (non-Jews), although that may not be too clear if you don't know where Gennesaret is, or Bethsaida. Geographical distinctions and recurring events suggest two subsections: a first journey and a second journey. I'll give you a bit of a geography lesson here so you can have a better idea of what's going on.

The following map shows the place names mentioned in Mark's Gospel. All the territory shown is at the eastern end of the Mediterranean Sea. Diagonal lines mark the Sea of Galilee and the Dead Sea. The dark line that runs down from the Sea of Galilee to the Dead Sea represents the Jordan River. The Sea of Galilee is a large, inland, freshwater lake. The Dead Sea is even larger but also an inland lake. It is

35

"dead," supporting no fish or plants, because it has no outlet; as water evaporates, the Dead Sea becomes saltier and saltier. On the west side of the Sea of Galilee is the Jewish region of Galilee, including the towns of Capernaum, Gennesaret, Dalmanutha (or Magdala), and Nazareth. The other side of the Sea of Galilee, the east side, is Gentile territory, including the cities of Caesarea Philippi and Bethsaida, "the country of the Gerasenes," and the region of the Decapolis (ten cities). Tyre and Sidon, north of Galilee, are in Syrophoenicia, also Gentile territory.

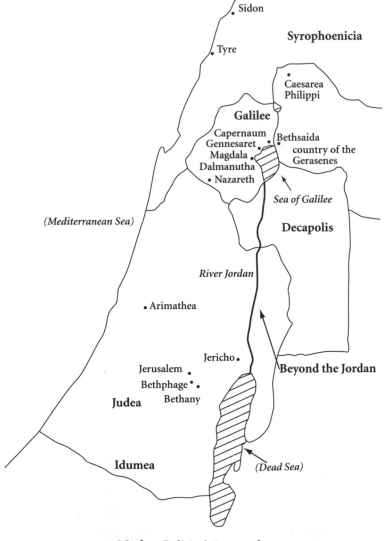

Markan Political Geography

Thus Jewish Galilee is "ringed" around by Gentiles; this appears to be the meaning of the name "Galilee." Judea, home region of the Jewish temple in Jerusalem, with its power and authority, is south of Galilee. Bethphage and Bethany are outlying villages of Jerusalem. Jericho and Arimathea are further out from the Jewish center of Jerusalem. This basic geography will be enough to enable us to follow Jesus' journeying in Mark 4:35-8:26.

FIRST JOURNEY (MARK 4:35–6:44)

The story begins with Jesus saying, "Let's go across to the other side." We're starting out in Jewish Galilee, so if we go across to the other side, it will be to Gentile territory.

Stilling the Storm (Mark 4:35–41)

Unfortunately, as Jesus and his disciples are on the Sea of Galilee— which is not really a sea but a large, freshwater lake—a great windstorm arises. The disciples are really worried; they think the boat is going to sink; yet Jesus is asleep—on a pillow. Jesus is not at all disturbed by the storm. In fact, the disciples have to wake him up, crying, "Jesus, don't you care that we are perishing?" Jesus says, "Peace. Be still," and the wind immediately ceases. Then he says to them, "Have you still no faith?" Faith means trust. Jesus seems to imply, "Don't you have any trust that you're going to be cared for? I'm telling you that God has come near, that the kingdom of God is breaking in, and you're worried about the wind?" The disciples respond, "Wow! Who is this? Who is this that even the wind and the sea obey him?" Pay close attention to the questions in the text of Mark. When there's a question that's not answered in the narrative, you know that the question is being forwarded to you. If no one in the story answers the question, then that's one the narrator is giving to the audience. (A storyteller or oral presenter would add the appropriate look and gesture.) So, who is this that even the wind and the sea obey him? We know that God gave dominion over the land to Adam and Eve, but God never gave dominion over the water to anyone. Only God can order the chaos of the sea.

Casting Out Demons (Mark 5:1–20)

With Jesus' godly intervention, the disciples do get safely to the other side, to the country of the Gerasenes in Gentile territory. There they meet a man with an unclean spirit, who's not really living with human beings any more; he lives among the tombs, among the dead. People have bound him with chains as if he's an animal, and he lives among the tombs as though he's dead. When he comes to Jesus, the unclean spirits within him say, "What have you to do with me, Jesus, Son of the Most High God?" Jesus asks, "What's your name?" The demons answer, "Legion." There's a joke here. Do you know what a legion is? A Roman legion? A division of the Roman army, the foreign army of occupation. The Roman legions, who patrolled Palestine in the time of Jesus, are being labeled as demonic.

Now suppose you don't know your geography very well, and you forget which side of the sea you are on. Well, here come some pigs, a large herd of swine. Because pigs are considered unclean animals by Jews, there is no need of pigs in Jewish Galilee. So the pigs really have to be over on the Gentile side. Just in case you get the geography a little confused, Mark always gives a second cue as to the surroundings. The pigs are, of course, an integral part of the story because the demons negotiate with Jesus to be sent into the pigs after being cast out of the man. But where do the pigs go? Whoosh! They rush down the bank into the sea and are drowned. "Legion" turns out to be violently self-destructive; perhaps the Roman empire will be so as well.

The Gerasenes want Jesus to leave. They don't want him destroying their economy. They don't want trouble. The healed man, however, wants to go with Jesus, wants to be with him. Jesus has already chosen twelve others to be with him, so he says, "No, you go home, home to your friends, and tell them how much the Lord has done for you." Jesus means for the man to go home to his circle of family and friends and tell them what the Lord God has done for him. Does the man obey? Well, it depends on what counts as obedience. Remember that the man is in the country of the Gerasenes. (Although scholars are not entirely sure where that is, it is clearly the area around one town near the east coast of the Sea of Galilee.) That's where his friends are too. But the healed man goes off to the Decapolis, to the ten *(deca)* Greek cities *(polis)*. He goes to the whole large area east and south of the Sea of Galilee, telling how much *Jesus* has done for him! Jesus said "Lord." The man said "Jesus." Is the Markan author leading his audience to confess that Jesus is Lord? Probably.

Healing a Woman and a Girl (Mark 5:21–43)

Then Jesus and the disciples cross again to the other side of the sea, to the west side. In case you get mixed up about where you are, here comes Jairus, one of the leaders of the synagogue. Does that tell you where you are? Where there are pigs, there are no synagogues; where there are synagogues, there are no pigs. Jairus, one of the leaders of the synagogue, comes to Jesus and says, "My daughter is at the point of death. So, please, come, and come now, and heal her." And Jesus agrees to come.

Well, there's a great crowd around Jesus, and they're pressing on him. Unexpectedly another scene intrudes. There's a woman in the crowd who has been hemorrhaging for twelve years. She's gone to many doctors, and she's only gotten worse, not better. That happens sometimes. But she says to herself, "If I touch even his clothes, I'll be made well." She trusts that just touching his clothes will be enough, so she reaches out and touches his cloak. And Jesus says, in the middle of the crowd, "Who touched my clothes?" His disciples say, "Are you kidding? What do you mean who touched your clothes? You're right in the middle of the crowd. We can't possibly tell who touched you." Yet Jesus says, "It wasn't that kind of touch. I'm talking about a really serious touch here. I felt the power go out from me." Of course, the woman hears this, and she's afraid; so she kneels down in front of Jesus and tells him the whole truth. She tells him exactly what she's done. Basically Jesus says, "Amazing! Your faith has made you well." Remember faith means trust; faith is not a head thing, not intellectual assent to propositions. Faith is an existential commitment. She threw her whole self into this trust in him. Jesus calls her "daughter," which is a significant part of the story because, in the eyes of some Jews (interpreting Leviticus 15:25–30), she probably would have been regarded as continually unclean due to her continual flow of blood. Jesus calls her "daughter," and that social reintegration may be as important as the physical healing.

Meanwhile, back at Jairus's house, the daughter, who was reported to be at the point of death five verses ago, has now died. Persons from Jairus's house come and say, "Don't trouble the teacher any further. Your daughter has died." Jesus hears this and says, "Have faith. You saw this woman; you saw her faith; you have that kind of faith. Don't fear; have trust." So they keep going, and Jesus takes three of his disciples, not the whole crew, and the parents, and goes in to the little girl, who's clearly dead. He says to her, "Talitha cum," which is Aramaic. (Jesus probably spoke Aramaic, but the Gospels are in Greek; however, occasionally a few words of Aramaic are sprinkled in.) "Talitha cum" means

"Little girl, get up." And you know what? She does. She gets up and she walks; at this point we find out she was twelve years old. (When I began reading this story for the first time as a child, I imagined this "little daughter" as an infant—perhaps because at that time twelve years old seemed "big" to me! Now that I have a twelve-year-old daughter, I realize that "little" is the parent's term of endearment.)

A few verses later Jesus says, "Give her something to eat." If she can walk and eat, she's really alive again. Then—and this is incredible—the narrator says Jesus "strictly ordered them that no one should know this." Now at the very beginning of the story the narrator reported weeping and wailing and a great commotion; that was the beginning of the funeral! Imagine, you're attending a funeral, and, all of a sudden, there's no corpse. The person got well and went home. Someone would have to tell the funeral director, "We've got to call this off." In Mark's story, the messianic secret is still in force. Characters are told, "Don't tell the story of Jesus yet because you don't know the whole story. Beware of the half truth; you may have hold of the wrong half. Don't tell *just* that Jesus brings people back to life. There's more to it." But, of course, this news can't be held in; it's just like new wine—it can't be held in old wineskins.

The two stories are sandwiched together:

5:21–24   Jairus's request for healing his daughter
5:25–34   healing of the hemorrhaging woman
5:35–43   raising of Jairus's daughter

This arrangement has occurred before in Mark, and it will occur again. It's a good technique for listening. A-B-A. You make a connection. The kind of faith that the woman has is the kind of faith that Jairus will also need. The two stories are also linked by the number twelve— twelve years of suffering for the woman, twelve years of living for the girl. Twelve, a subtle allusion to the twelve tribes of Israel, reinforces the Jewish context of the two stories. In addition, Jesus restores both the woman and the girl to potential life-giving roles. The woman's reproductive system is restored to health; the girl, at the threshold of puberty (and, in the ancient world, marriage), lives to enter womanhood.

Jesus in His Hometown (Mark 6:1–6a)

Jesus now goes to his hometown. Perhaps the audience is thinking, "Maybe they'll have a parade. Hometown boy makes good!" The people Jesus grew up with ask really good questions. But the questions aren't answered, so whom are they for? They're for you. "Where did this man get all this? What is this wisdom that has been given to him? What deeds of power are being done by his hands!" (NRSV). All very good questions. The hometown crowd knows the power is not from within Jesus himself alone. Where did he get it? The wisdom is coming from someplace else. Where's it coming from? The deeds of power are by his hands but not from his energy. Where's it coming from? But then the final question shows that it is impossible for Jesus' compatriots to see the implications of their first three questions. "Isn't he a carpenter, the son of Mary, whose brothers and sisters we know? His family's not that great, so how can he be anything?"

Bridging the gap between the implications of their first three questions and their fourth, Jesus asserts, "Prophets are not without honor, except in their own hometown." The saying is probably not original with Jesus; it's probably a cliché. But it certainly fits the story. The narrator reports, "Jesus could do no deed of power there—well, except that he healed a few." (Perhaps this is like Jesus being alone—except for the twelve and those who were around him.) The narrator says that Jesus is amazed at their unfaith, their untrust. Normally a healing story concludes with a statement that "they all were amazed at what had happened." Here Jesus is amazed at what can't happen when there's no trust.

Sending Out the Twelve (Mark 6:6b–13)

So Jesus goes on among the villages teaching. He realizes the time has come to increase his ability to reach people by sending out the disciples. So he sends them out two by two to have authority over the unclean spirits. He gives explicit instructions: They can take a staff; they can take sandals, but they can't take bread—no bread, no bag, no money. They are to go where they're welcome, and if they're not welcome, they are to leave the place, even leaving their dust behind by shaking it off their feet before going on to the next place. And so they do. They all go out, and they proclaim that all should repent—like John went out and proclaimed that all should repent, and like Jesus went out and proclaimed that all should repent. And they cast out many demons—like Jesus had cast out many demons. They even do something that had not been reported of Jesus: they anoint with oil many that are sick. Such anointing was apparently practiced in Mark's community, making this a "you were there" story. Were you there when they crucified our Lord?

Were you there when they anointed the sick with oil? The boundary between the characters and the audience is a semipermeable membrane. Do you remember what Jesus' disciples were called to do? To be with Jesus and to be sent out to preach and to have authority to cast out demons. And that's exactly what they're doing here. Having been with Jesus (since chapter 1), and having been commissioned by him (in chapter 3), they are sent out and extend his ministry of preaching and healing (in chapter 6).

Death of John (Mark 6:14–29)

Then there's a strange transition. It seems that Herod heard about these things, about Jesus and the disciples. So Herod and others have a little conversation about who they think Jesus is. Some think he is Elijah or one of the other prophets. But Herod, who has cause to be feeling guilty, says, "Oh, no! He's got to be John the Baptist, whom I beheaded, raised up." Then there's a flashback to Herod's beheading of John. It seems there was trouble between John and Herod and Herodias because of their marriage; Herod was married to Herodias. The problem was that Herodias was previously married to Philip, who was Herod's brother. John insisted that Herod shouldn't be married to his brother's wife, and John was imprisoned for his critique. But Herodias and Herod feel very differently about John. Herod is perplexed because he's attracted to John; he likes to listen to him. Herodias feels no such attraction. Later, there's a birthday party for Herod, who seems to have a bit too much wine—at least he becomes less than his best rational self.

As part of the celebration, Herodias's daughter, Herod's stepdaughter, dances. Herodias's daughter is also named Herodias in this story; in other stories she's named Salome, which is easier, but here we've got Herodias, Herodias, and Herod. Herod is pleased, very pleased with the dance and the daughter. Extravagantly he tells the daughter, "You can have anything you want, even up to half of my kingdom." He says this in front of his guests, so to keep his honor he has to keep his word. Daughter Herodias runs to mother Herodias and asks, "Mom, what should I get? What should I ask for?" Mom suggests, "The head of John the Baptist." Daughter requests, "The head of John the Baptist on a platter." Maybe she's going to keep the platter. So here at the feast they bring in a final nonedible dish—the head of John the Baptist on a platter! After that gruesome scene, the end of the story is touching. At the end John's disciples come and take his body and lay it in a tomb. That's what disciples do when their master is dead; they come and take his body and lay it in a tomb.

Return of the Twelve (Mark 6:30)

Meanwhile Jesus' disciples come back. They were sent out before the narration of the story of John (which, of course, had happened sometime earlier). Now they come back and tell Jesus all they've done. And what is it they have done? And what is it Mark is doing? Mark tells us about the sending out of the disciples, then John's death, then the disciples' return. A-B-A. John went out and preached, and he was arrested and later killed. Jesus went out and preached, and he was rejected and. . . . The disciples go out and preach, and. . . . Whoa! You know, if you were one of the disciples you'd begin to be worried about the pattern that is beginning to become clear here.

Feeding Five Thousand (Mark 6:31–44)

Jesus and the disciples are tired; they are trying to get away. So they find a boat and go to a deserted place, or what they think is a deserted place. It's not across the sea. And how do we know that? Because the next verse says the crowd beat them there on foot. Even though Jesus walks on water, the whole crowd does not! So Jesus and the disciples are still on the west side, the Jewish side of the Sea of Galilee. They try to get away, and they can't get away; they go out into the wilderness. This is not the wilderness today's conservationists seek to preserve. The Greek term used here, *erēmos,* does not mean a natural environment that has been spared destructive human intervention; it means a place that does not sustain human life, a deserted place. Yet all these people are there in the wilderness listening. Jesus teaches them because he knows they're like sheep without a shepherd, which is a common Jewish image of the people of God without a leader. Jesus is performing the role of the shepherd for them by teaching them.

It gets to be late. The disciples say, "Send them away; too many people here to feed. Send them away so that they can get something to eat." Jesus says, "No, you feed them. You feed them." They respond, "Are you kidding? There are thousands of people here. It would take 200 denarii, two hundred days' wages, just to buy enough bread to feed these people!" But Jesus says, "Start with what you've got. I don't want any sad stories or excuses. Always, always, always, start with what you've got. And what have you got? Take inventory. Okay. Five loaves and two fish. That's a start." So Jesus takes the loaves, and he blesses the loaves, and he breaks the loaves, and he gives the loaves. And he feeds the people, and he feeds them, and he feeds them. All the people eat and are satisfied. (This shared meal offers a striking contrast with Herod's banquet for the powerful and their retainers.) When the people are finished, Jesus tells his disciples, "Pick up the leftovers and put them into baskets." Remarkably they have twelve baskets full of leftover pieces. Remember that. And five thousand people were fed bread in the wilderness.

SECOND JOURNEY (MARK 6:45–8:26)

A second journey begins with a new destination.

Walking on the Sea (Mark 6:45–52)

Then Jesus says to his disciples, "Go on ahead of me to the other side of the sea, to Bethsaida. Go over to Bethsaida, where there are Gentiles. I'm going to pray on the mountain; I need to communicate with God." So they go onto the sea, and they're rowing, but they're not getting anywhere because the wind is coming up again. You know, the sea is kind of tough on these guys. So early in the morning Jesus notices and, although he comes near to them, he intends to pass them by. It's as if he's just coming to see if they're okay. You know what you do with a toddler? You wonder, can she really do this by herself? I'll just stand nearby and see. If she's okay, I'll leave her alone, but if she really needs help, I'll be there. It seems almost like that here.

The disciples see Jesus, think he's a ghost, and are, naturally enough, afraid. Jesus says, "Oh, don't be afraid; take heart." Then he says, "I am." I know the NRSV says, "It is I" because that's better grammar. But "I am" is the literal translation and has the better allusion. "I am" is God's response to Moses at the burning bush in the story in Exodus (3:1–6). Most people in Mark's audience would recognize that. Of course, the one who says "I am" here is Jesus, not God. We don't hear the disciples' words in the narrative, but they've got to be asking themselves, "Who is this? Who is this that talks like God? That acts like God?" What we do hear from the narrator about their response is this: "They were utterly astounded, for they did not understand about the loaves." That's a bit strange. It would seem more obvious to say, "They were utterly astounded because of the miracle—you know, walking on water." Oh, no, what they didn't understand was the loaves. And they didn't understand because "their hearts were hardened." The audience steeped in biblical stories would recognize the allusion to Pharaoh's hardened heart. Mark is leading them to make connections: Bread in the desert. A water miracle. Going through the sea as if it were dry land. Hardened hearts. There are too many coincidences here. This story has exodus written all over it—exodus, that great moment when God acted for the people of God to bring them out of slavery into freedom. So what is God bringing these people out of now? What is God bringing these people into here?

Healing Many (Mark 6:53–56)

Do you remember where the disciples were headed in the boat? Over to the other side, to Bethsaida. But they land at Gennesaret, which is still on the west side, the Jewish side, of the Sea of Galilee. Apparently they get blown off course because of the wind that made it impossible to row. They don't go where they were sent; they land in home territory. There, in familiar territory, the narrator presents a familiar story: Jesus heals many people. Whoever touches even the fringe of Jesus' garment, probably the fringe of his Jewish prayer shawl, is healed.

Challenging Tradition (Mark 7:1–13)

Then, just in case we are mixed up about which side we're on, the Pharisees show up. The Pharisees, who have authority in the synagogue, are on the side where there are synagogues. Here the Pharisees are joined by scribes who have come down from Jerusalem, the Jewish religious and political center. (One always comes *down* from Jerusalem, even when traveling north to Galilee, because of the higher elevation of Jerusalem, a well-chosen spot for the temple.) The Pharisees and scribes see that the disciples of Jesus are eating with unwashed hands. They're not worried about germs; they're worried about the ritual of washing hands to separate the sacred and the profane. Then the narrator gives an aside for those in the audience who aren't Jewish, explaining what the Pharisees do and what the Jews do concerning traditions of washing. This aside tells us that not everyone in the community for whom this story was told was Jewish. It doesn't necessarily tell us that no one in the audience was Jewish, even though Jewish tradition is being challenged. Probably the community behind Mark's Gospel was a mixed community of Jewish and Gentile believers in the Christ. When Jewish tradition is challenged here, it is on the basis of Jewish Scripture. It's an inside critique.

The Pharisees and scribes challenge Jesus, "Why do your disciples—and why do you let your disciples—disregard the tradition of the elders?" Jesus responds, "Because I'm really busy getting them to pay attention to something else—like the commandment of God." Then Jesus returns the challenge: "You abandon the commandment of God and hold to your own tradition. Moses said, 'Honor your father and mother.' But you have a tradition that says, if money or property is declared by its owner to be 'Corban'—'dedicated' to God—then that money cannot be used for a secular purpose. That may sound nice, but, if taking care of one's parents is dismissed as a secular purpose, this tradition is in conflict with the law given through Moses. Thus you are using this community rule to get away from God's rules for community, which must have priority."

It is worth noting that no other evidence of the ruling attributed to the Pharisees in this Markan story exists. In addition, the judgment given in a case similar to this one in the Mishnah, a codification of Jewish teaching made after the Gospels were written, agrees with the attitude of Jesus as depicted in Mark. This situation reminds us that Mark's Gospel is a proclamation of the "good news" about Jesus, not a documentary about first-century Judaism.

Inside Out (Mark 7:14–23)

Then Jesus calls the crowd to him, not just the scribes and Pharisees, but the crowd, saying, "You know, nothing outside of a person going inside of a person makes a person defiled. It's the things that are inside a person that come out of a person that make a person defiled." The narrator makes the implication of this explicit in a parenthetical aside: "Thus he declared all foods clean." A serious debate about religious practice is reflected here. Traditional Jewish food laws served to reinforce strict boundaries between Jews and Gentiles as insiders and outsiders. The issue at stake here concerning food will soon be raised in other ways concerning bread.

After presenting the parable to the crowd, Jesus goes into a house with the disciples. They ask him concerning this parable, and Jesus responds, "Then you also can't understand? To you has been given the mystery of this kingdom of God, and you aren't supposed to be outsiders, but you aren't catching on any better than those who are outside. Sometimes I have to wonder. This is the way it is: Food is what comes from outside of your body, goes inside of your body, goes through your digestive tract, and—to put it directly—goes out into the latrine. And none of that defiles you. So it doesn't matter what you eat—or what others eat. What defiles you is what is inside, in your heart: the evil intentions that lead to fornication, theft, murder, adultery, greed; all of those evil thoughts and actions that come out of you—that defiles you; that makes you unclean—whether you're Jewish or Gentile."

Healing Another Daughter (Mark 7:24–30)

Since the conversation about defilement began with Pharisees and scribes, the action would be over in Jewish territory, over in Galilee. Jesus is still trying to get away. He's always trying to get away in this section, but he never actually succeeds. Now he says, "Let's go north. Let's go up to Gentile territory; no Pharisees are going to come up there, so that will be safe. Let's go to Tyre," which is north along the coast, in Syrophoenicia. So Jesus goes to a private house way up in Tyre, trying to hide, but even there he cannot be hid.

A Syrophoenician woman comes to the house, a Greek woman, and she says, "I want you to heal my daughter." Perhaps the first thing you think is "Oh, Jesus likes daughters! I mean, he healed Jairus's daughter; he more than healed Jairus's daughter; he raised her up after she had already died. So Jesus likes daughters, and this is going to be another successful healing story." But Jesus rebuffs the mother! The audience is surprised. Jesus says, "Let the children be fed first, for it's not fair to take the children's food and throw it to the dogs." Who's he calling a dog? Who are the children? Clearly the Jews are the children. The foreign woman who wants Jesus' help is called a dog. But if she's a dog, she yaps right back. She says, "Okay. You want to do metaphors? I can do metaphors. Sir, even the dogs under the table get the children's crumbs. I have one little Gentile girl here. You've got enough power to heal her. You can do that. You can be inclusive enough; you can heal this daughter of mine as you healed Jairus's daughter. There's enough of you to go around." Jesus responds, "I'm impressed. What you say brings me up short. For this *logos*, for this saying, you may go; you may go because the demon has left your daughter."

Now the audience is also amazed. The Markan Jesus is shown as learning from a Gentile woman about inclusive community, and that's probably more startling than anything else in the story—that Jesus is shifting his position here on the basis of this woman's powerful metaphoric argument. It's almost as if she's saying to Jesus, "Well, start with what you've got." She's stretching what Jesus has proclaimed elsewhere to a broader context. "Start with what you've got. It's probably going to be enough." Jesus has ears to hear her.

Healing a Deaf Man (Mark 7:31–37)

Mark 7:31 has got to be the strangest geographical reference in the text. It says that Jesus returned from the region of Tyre and went by way of Sidon, which sounds okay because Tyre and Sidon always go together in biblical tradition. The problem is that Sidon is further north. So he's returning south by going further north; that's a peculiar start. (I have a similar problem in reverse when flying: I have to fly south from Roanoke, Virginia, to Atlanta, to fly north to Boston!) He's going out of the way; he returns (presumably to Galilee, to the south) from the region of Tyre (in the north), by way of Sidon (further north), toward the Sea of Galilee (to the south and east), through the region of the Decapolis (further south and east). And where does he end up? We don't know why the route is so messy, but Jesus does seem to end up in the Decapolis, over among the ten Greek cities, definitely Gentile territory.

As soon as he arrives, a deaf man with a speech impediment is brought to Jesus for healing. Jesus takes him aside privately, not to be observed, and he heals him using Greco-Roman healing techniques— touching and spitting. Spitting is not a technique that Jewish healers normally use; fluids that come out of the body can render the person ritually unclean for a time. So this is the second cue that we're among Gentiles—that Jesus is using a healing technique acceptable among Gentiles. This second cue about locale is especially appreciated after the confusing travel note in 7:31. But Jesus also speaks an Aramaic word, which here in Gentile territory is a foreign language, and a foreign language has power. He says, "Ephphatha," "Be opened." Not only can the man hear, but he can speak. Jesus ordered them to tell no one, but the more he ordered it, the more zealously they proclaimed it. Jesus tries to keep a lid on his healing activity, but that is not going to happen. The audience inside the story is saying, "He has done everything well; he even makes the deaf to hear and the mute to speak." Now this is a Jewish messianic expectation, but it's over in the Gentile Decapolis that people are saying it. So what is happening here? The Jewish Messiah is over there healing the Gentiles? The Jewish Messiah is in foreign territory healing outsiders?

Feeding Four Thousand (Mark 8:1–9)

And while he's over there somewhere, presumably still in the Decapolis because the narrator doesn't supply a geographical reference to tell us otherwise, Jesus has compassion for the hungry crowd. There's no reference to an image from Jewish Scripture (sheep without a shepherd) this time. Jesus' motivation is human compassion; if he sends the people home hungry they will faint on the way. The disciples ask, "How can we feed all these people with bread in the wilderness? " The audience outside the story thinks, "Wait a minute! Just a few verses back Jesus fed thousands of people with bread in the wilderness, and now the disciples are in the wilderness saying, 'What are we going to do?'" And Jesus says, "Start with what you've got. What do you have this time?" Now they have seven loaves. So Jesus takes the loaves, and he blesses the loaves, and he breaks the loaves, and he gives the loaves.

Do you hear an echo here? He did this before. He took, and he blessed, and he broke, and he gave. These four verbs occur one more time in Mark—at the Last Supper. At table with his disciples, Jesus takes the bread, and he blesses the bread, and he breaks the bread, and he gives the bread. It's another way the early Christians would have said, "We were there." They'd say, "We do that; we do that every time we come together on the Lord's Day. We take the bread, and we bless the bread, and we break the bread, and we give the bread." In the early Christian church the feeding stories, the stories of Jesus' miraculous multiplication of bread, were understood as eucharistic, as communion references, as pointers to the celebration of the Lord's Supper. Again there are leftovers; this time seven baskets full. Remember that. And four thousand people were fed bread in the wilderness—four thousand Gentiles. The Markan Jesus lives up to the Syrophoenician woman's faith: there is plenty of bread for everyone, more than crumbs for all who are hungry.

Refusing a Request for a Sign (Mark 8:10–12)

Then Jesus and the disciples are back in the boat, and they go over to Dalmanutha, on the Jewish side. (Actually we don't know exactly where Dalmanutha was because we never found a sign that says, "Dalmanutha was here." It's probably where Magdala was, the town of

Mary of Magdala, Mary Magdalene.) There the Pharisees come and ask for a sign to test him. Our first reaction might be to think, "Where have these guys been? What further sign could they want beyond walking on water, calming the sea, healing the sick, and multiplying the loaves?" But in Mark's Gospel, "sign" is not used in a positive sense; Jesus only uses it in a negative sense. "Why does this generation want a sign?" Jesus asks, implying perhaps, "You want magic. You want God in a box. You want something nice and unambiguous. Sorry, wrong Messiah. I'm an ambiguous Messiah; there's going to be no unambiguous sign, and anybody who's going to be my follower will have to deal with that."

Questions on the Sea (Mark 8:13–21)

Then Jesus and the disciples are back in the boat. That was short! It's almost as if they went to the other side, the Jewish side, just for that brief conversation with the Pharisees. So they're back in the boat again, going to the other side, that is, the Gentile side. The disciples have forgotten to bring bread, having only one loaf. This is funnier in Greek because the term "bread" is the same as "loaves": they didn't have any "loaves"; they had only one "loaf." Jesus says, "Watch out—beware of the yeast of the Pharisees and the yeast of Herod." The disciples respond, "We don't have any bread. So why should we watch out for the yeast? The yeast is in the loaves, and we don't have any loaves." Jesus responds, perhaps with a sigh, "Why are you talking about bread? You know, you've got to extend your mind beyond the literal if you're ever going to understand anything serious in life. Do you still not perceive or understand? Are you like those to whom Isaiah prophesied? Are your hearts still hardened like Pharaoh's? What have you learned? We've spent all this time together, and what have you learned? Let's take this once more from the top. Disciples, do you remember at the feeding of the five thousand, how many baskets were left over?" "We know that. That was twelve, right?" "Do you remember how many baskets were left over when we fed the four thousand?" "We know that. We know that too. That was seven." Then Jesus says to them, "Do you not yet understand?" Many of my students say this is the point where they really identify with the disciples—because they don't understand either!

But had you been in Mark's community you would have known the symbolism of numbers. You would have known that twelve is the number of Israel. How many disciples were there? Twelve. How old was Jairus's daughter? Twelve. How many years had the woman been hemorrhaging? Twelve. And were these characters on the Jewish side? They were. Twelve is a Jewish number because of the twelve tribes. Seven is a little harder. According to Jewish calculations, there are seventy nations of the Gentiles, of the "others." There's the one nation of the Jews, and there are seventy nations of the *ethnoi,* the ethnic groups, the peoples, the nations. There's a story in Acts in which the twelve Jewish disciples need some help among the Greeks, so seven deacons are appointed. Seven, seventy—it's the number for everybody; it's the universal number. Seven days of the week, seven planetary deities, seven seas, seven continents, seven hills of Rome—seven is the number of completeness. Twelve and seven are absolutely basic.

Reviewing Mark 4:35–8:22a—Journeys and Community

"Do you not yet understand?" The question is not answered by the disciples, so it's forwarded to you, the audience. You have to reflect. Whom does Jesus feed? Whom does Jesus heal? Whom does Jesus teach? Both Jews and Gentiles. Both insiders and outsiders. Were the disciples able to go over to Gentile territory when they were sent? No; when they were sent to Gentile Bethsaida they landed at Jewish Gennesaret. Were the disciples able to envision an inclusive community beyond the boundaries of their own group? Perhaps not. But was Jesus able to lead them there, lead them beyond the boundaries of their own group? At 8:22 the narrator says, "And they came to Bethsaida." I think most contemporary readers just ignore the place names—unless they have to pronounce them in reading Scripture in worship. Since we don't usually know where the places are, it is easier to assume they're not really relevant to the story. But we miss a lot that way. Consider this pattern. The Markan Jesus directed the disciples (at 6:45), "Go; go beyond your own group; go out to the world and proclaim the good news of the in-breaking of God's kingdom." And they couldn't do it on their own. So he said, "All right. I'll go with you. We'll do this together one more time—healing Gentiles, feeding Gentiles, teaching Gentiles. We will get to Bethsaida, if not by sea then by an overland detour, but it will be worth the delay." The Markan narrator reports (at 8:22), "And they came to Bethsaida."

Healing a Blind Man (Mark 8:22–26)

And there in Bethsaida a blind man is brought to Jesus. Jesus puts saliva (second cue of the Gentile setting) on his fingers, touches them to the man's eyes, and says, "Can you see anything?" The man says, "Hmm.

Sort of. I see people, but they look like trees walking." (When he was young, my son observed, "Well, then the man wasn't born blind." That's right. It doesn't say he was born blind; that story's in John 9.) This man apparently could once see; he knows what trees look like, he knows what people look like, and what he sees is a cross between the two. So Jesus puts his hands on him again, and his sight is restored, and he sees clearly, and he says, "The trees are standing still now; only the people are walking." And Jesus says, "Do not even enter the village. This will create a big stir. My work cannot keep quiet if you don't keep quiet."

The audience might wonder, "Is Jesus' power slipping? It took him two tries to heal this man." Neither Matthew nor Luke, who were probably using Mark, pick up the story. But I don't really think they didn't like the story; I think they knew it was Mark's special story. I think they knew very well how this story was working in Mark's Gospel, but they each had their own stories to tell. They surely realized that the story of the healing of blindness had a deeper meaning. Such symbolism is all over the ancient world. Have you ever read *Oedipus Rex (Oedipus the King)*? When does Oedipus blind himself? When he finally sees. Tiresias, the prophet, who sees from the beginning, is blind. The blind see, and the seeing become blind. So, in addition to the literal meaning, there's a symbolic meaning.

Do the disciples see everything clearly all the time? Not exactly. Do they sort of see trees walking? They see healing for Jews, bread for Jews, teaching for Jews. But do they see clearly beyond that? Jesus has to heal their blindness by stages. Healing also for Gentiles, bread also for Gentiles, teaching also for Gentiles. Are there any more stages of insight? That's a question for the next section. Begin your reading of Mark's chapters 8 through 10 with that very question.

Reviewing Mark 4:35–8:26—Community

What we've seen in chapters 4 through 8 of Mark is Jesus healing and feeding on both sides of the sea. The sea is not where people live; it's a boundary. The Jordan River and the Sea of Galilee are the boundaries between the Jewish territory of Galilee and Gentile territory. The water is a boundary—and a problem—for those on the land on either side. But not for Jesus. The disciples can't make it across the sea *with* the boat; Jesus doesn't even need the boat to cross the sea. On the sea Jesus acts with the power of God—calming the sea, walking on the water. Jesus has proclaimed that God has come near. On the land Jesus acts with the power of God—providing bread for all—across the boundaries that humans have made.

What are Jesus' followers to understand and to do about this reign or *kingdom* of God that is breaking in (the focus of the previous chapter of this guide)? And what are they to think and do about this *community* (present chapter focus) that gathers in anticipation of the kingdom? The community must both anticipate and reflect what's happening in the kingdom. For Mark's community, the Jewish/Gentile boundary was a crucial *internal* boundary. The early community of believers in the Christ included Jews and Gentiles. The early hope for an inclusive community of Jews and Gentiles reflected in Mark's Gospel has not materialized in the subsequent history of Christianity. Hearing Mark's Gospel reminds us of that high hope and critiques our lesser reality.

But because the Jewish/Gentile boundary was internal to Mark's community, it is also appropriate for those of us who hear Mark's Gospel in the Christian community today to ask, what are our internal boundaries? Because Jews and Gentiles were really in Mark's own house, hearing Mark's Gospel must raise for us questions about the boundaries that separate us from those in our own house. What are the things that divide Christians from Christians? Race? Class? Gender? Ethnicity? Money? Ideology? All of these things? Where are we seeing trees walking? Where is our blindness in need of a second stage of healing?

> *O God,*
> *that we, like Jesus, might be brothers and sisters*
> *with all your people,*
> *give us ears to hear the Gospel of Mark*
> *as good news for an inclusive community*
> *beyond the boundaries that restrict our love.*
> *Amen.*

Discipleship

Mark 8:22–10:52

O God,
whose way we, like Jesus, seek to follow,
give us ears to hear the Gospel of Mark
as good news of daring discipleship
that manifests your love in startling ways
in the world.
Amen.

It's not a typographical error that there is slight overlap in the verses discussed in the previous chapter and in this chapter. That's intentional. There is one story here that really fits tightly both with what it follows and with what it precedes. It's the conclusion to part two and the introduction to part three.

Before looking at that special story, I want to say something about the two halves of Mark's Gospel. The half we've been looking at, chapters 1 through 8, shows a Jesus of power. He speaks powerfully; he heals people; he casts out demons. But he's always saying, "Don't tell, don't tell, don't tell what you know." And what do we know? We know that he is a Jesus of power. There are two major questions: Who is Jesus? and Who are the disciples? And these two questions go together. In the ancient world everybody knew that if a person had followers, their lives would be similar to their leader's life. That's what it meant to follow somebody—to have the same pattern of life. So if you know what Jesus was like, then you know what his followers should be like as well.

When we look at the second half of the Gospel, chapters 8 through 16, we get a very different picture of Jesus from that painted in chapters 1 through 8. You would think people who are in power would not have to suffer, and people in power are usually served by others. But, in fact, this view is turned topsy-turvy in Mark's Gospel. In effect Jesus says, "The kind of Christ I am is one who serves—and ends up suffering, not because I'm really into suffering but because sometimes that happens when you challenge the status quo. When you serve people who don't have power, sometimes people who do have power react badly against you. So sometimes suffering is a consequence of that kind of service."

This model stands in contrast to a number of "divine men" that one hears stories about in the ancient world—humans who share in some divine power. In that world, Jesus is not the only healer; he's not the only strong teacher. There were others who could heal the sick and cast out demons—for example, Apollonius of Tyana, a neo-Pythagorean teacher and holy man. Such powers weren't that unusual, although they were often manifest in persons of higher social status than Jesus. The Roman historian Tacitus tells of healings accomplished by the emperor Vespasian. Jesus is from Nazareth, a little bump on a log of a town; that was pretty odd for a healer. But it wasn't odd to be a healer. Still, most healers were powerful people who weren't usually personally involved in service or suffering. So some scholars think Mark's Gospel keeps saying, "Don't tell, don't tell" because the audience might get Jesus mixed up with one of these "divine men"—unless they hear the whole story. If they hear the whole story, then they'll see that he's really quite different. But one has to hear the whole story before coming to a conclusion.

Mark 8:22–10:52 is one of the first sections about which scholars began to think, "That's put together rather well." In the "old days," in the eighteenth century, scholars used to view Mark's Gospel as kind of rough and ready. At the level of the sentence, it seems to have some grammatical errors; the way it uses verb tenses—switching from past to present and back again—is a bit primitive; it's not as polished as Luke. Yet Mark's style is close to oral storytelling, and Mark's power comes at the level of the story. (And they "fix" all those so-called grammatical errors in the English translations anyway! In Mark's Greek text, sentences frequently begin with *kai,* "and"; this conversational effect is nearly lost in the NRSV.) At the level of the story Mark is well organized. This section begins with the story of the healing of a blind man, and it ends with a story of the healing of a blind man; so it has a frame, like a picture frame all around. The middle is structured around three passion predictions: three times Jesus says, "The Son of Man is going to suffer and die and be raised again." Each passion prediction is followed by a misunderstanding by the disciples, which is, in turn, followed by Jesus' discipleship instruction. So we have a frame focused on blindness and sight, surrounding three lessons on discipleship. Other events are inserted, important events—the confession of Peter, the transfiguration, one exorcism, and a teaching section—but they serve as significant interludes in this other framework. Let's go through this structure.

FIRST LESSON (MARK 8:22–9:1)

We begin with a story we have already considered, "and they came to Bethsaida"!!! If you have read the previous chapter of this guide, you understand the exclamation marks. You know why it's such a big deal that they came to Bethsaida—because Bethsaida is over in Gentile territory where Jesus had tried to send the disciples earlier (at 6:45), and they couldn't make it alone. So he took them by the hand, and he led them all around, and finally "they came to Bethsaida." Eventually they made it together and broadened their community.

Healing a Blind Man (Mark 8:22–26)

At Bethsaida people bring a blind man to Jesus, and he heals him in two stages. In the first stage the man sees people, and they look like "trees walking." Then Jesus heals him again and he sees clearly. Though most scholars simply relate the two-stage healing to what happens after, if you were *hearing* it (think about that), you wouldn't know what happened after yet. In that case you might well connect it to what happened before—two stages: the Jewish stage and the Gentile stage, two stages of ministry, two stages of insight. The audience might be wondering, as I suggested before, Has Jesus' power slipped? Is he losing it if he can't heal the man in one try? Probably not. Probably it's symbolic. In the ancient world, sight/blindness stories were often symbolic. There are examples of blind prophets, like Tiresias, who could really "see," and people who could see, like Oedipus, who were "blind" to things around them. It's quite traditional. In Mark the two stages might be related to Jesus' ministry to the Jews and to the Gentiles. Jesus has been trying to heal the blindness of the disciples regarding these two stages. The story of the two-stage healing also raises the question of whether there are further stages of sight or insight to come.

Peter: "You Are the Christ" (Mark 8:27–30)

Then we move to a story that mentions "on the way" (8:27). This phrase occurs over and over again, but you could easily miss it in the New Revised Standard Version. You pick up a little more in the older Revised Standard Version. The translators are trying to be so good about avoiding word repetition in English that they use different phrases: "And as he was setting out on his journey," "And they were on the road." In Greek it's always the same: *en tē hodō* on the way. Here Jesus and the disciples are on the way to the villages of Caesarea Philippi.

Caesarea Philippi is the dominant town, with satellite villages around it. This is north of Bethsaida, in Gentile territory, on the other side, the east side, of the Sea of Galilee. So they're way up there. And Jesus asks, "Who do people say that I am?" His disciples answer, "Well, some say John the Baptist (we know that's what Herod thought; chapter 6); some say Elijah (also mentioned in chapter 6); some say one of the prophets." Jesus says, "Okay. Fine. Just getting you warmed up. But who do *you* say that I am?" That's what he really wants to know: "Who do *you* say that I am?" Peter is the one who speaks up—good, bad, but never indifferent; Peter speaks up, saying, "You are the Christ." We know, of course, that Christ is Messiah. It's not Jesus' last name; it's a title. Now think about this title for a moment. The Hebrew term *Messiah,* translated into Greek as *Christos* and into English as "Christ," is a title for the anointed one, one called by God and given a special task. Thus we who are called Christians are literally "Messiah-folk," anointed ones, people who fol-low one who has a special task and thereby also have a special task. So Christ-folk are Messiah-folk or anointed-folk.

We remember the title of Mark's Gospel, "The beginning of the gospel of Jesus Christ," and we think, "Aha! Peter identified Jesus as the Christ; the narrator identified Jesus as the Christ; that is the correct answer; Peter got it right." Yet Jesus "sternly ordered them not to tell anyone about him." The messianic secret par excellence: "Don't tell I am the Messiah. You just said I am the Messiah, but don't tell it." Peter is right, but you have to wonder if he's only seeing "trees walking." Does Peter really see clearly yet?

First Passion Prediction (Mark 8:31–32a)

In the next episode—and it's bam, just like that!—Jesus says, "Well, let me tell you something about the kind of Messiah I'm going to be. The Son of Man [a strange phrase, though it's clear the Markan Jesus uses it to refer to himself] is going to undergo suffering and rejection and be killed and after the third day rise again." Jesus says all this quite openly.

Misunderstanding (Mark 8:32b–33)

Then Peter, taking Jesus aside, responds, "Wait a second. I just said you were the Christ, the Messiah, but that is not what I meant. Suffering is not what I meant." So Peter rebukes Jesus. This is a strong word. Finally Jesus, turning to all the disciples, rebukes Peter. It is a mutual rebuking. Normally Jesus rebukes unclean spirits, so when he rebukes his own disciple and then calls him Satan ("Get behind me, Satan!") for not setting his mind on divine things but on human things, it's a big deal. I mean if I were Peter I would think, "What?! I just got the star question right, and now I'm in trouble? What happened?" Peter's confession has become Peter's confusion. We've changed gears; there's something new to learn here. We quickly learn that Peter does see "trees walking"; he sees a "trees walking" powerful Christ. He's taken hold of a half-truth, the wrong half. Yet Jesus is patient; we're going to go through this explanation again and give Peter another chance. It's clear from here that the human things Peter is thinking of involve power—powerful healing, powerful teaching; that's the human way of thinking. It's not yet clear what is the divine way of thinking; we have to keep going.

Discipleship Instruction (Mark 8:34–9:1)

Although Peter had taken Jesus aside privately, and Jesus had turned to all his disciples, now Jesus calls the whole crowd and says, "Everybody, come hear this: If any want to become my followers, let them deny themselves and take up their cross and follow me." The cross was a form of punishment and execution used by the Romans for political criminals, not for petty thieves, and not for religious offenders within the Jewish tradition. Crucifixion was for those challenging the Roman authority, challenging the status quo of the powerful. And Jesus says, "That's what you have to be willing to do. You have to be willing to challenge those in power if you want to follow me. For those who want to save their lives will end up losing them, and those willing to lose their lives—not for no reason, but for my sake and for the sake of the good news of God's in-breaking kingdom—will in fact find their lives." Quite paradoxical. No wonder Peter was having a bit of trouble catching on!

Then there are some more teachings. At this point it's almost as if Mark says, "Oh, I've got some other good teachings, and I need to stick them somewhere." It gets to be something of a scrapbook here. There are some sayings about what will happen "in the future." In the future you will see the Son of Man coming with the glory of the Father, and if you are ashamed of the Son of Man now, in that future he will be ashamed of you. And in the future you will see that the kingdom of God has come with power. In fact, there are some standing here who will not taste death before they see that—that the kingdom of God has, in fact, come with power. But now, now, you must be willing to suffer; you must be willing not to be powerful. You must be willing not to try to be like the powerful, but to serve.

Reviewing Mark 8:31–9:1—First Passion Prediction Unit

Here we have what scholars call a passion prediction unit, consisting of three parts: a passion prediction by Jesus, a misunderstanding by the disciples, and Jesus' instruction about discipleship. Here Jesus' discipleship instruction includes the crowd. The crowd is frequently our entrance into the story. When you read "the crowd," it seems that you must step right in at that point. You may step in at other points too, but you've got to step in at that point. Remember this pattern of a passion prediction unit; we'll hear it again.

SECOND LESSON (MARK 9:2–50)

With this lesson about Jesus' passion and their own discipleship behind them, Jesus and the disciples move on.

God: "This Is My Son" (Mark 9:2–13)

The narrator begins, "Six days later . . ." Six days later than what? Whatever. If you're familiar with biblical tradition, "six days later" reminds you of the story in Exodus 24:15–18 where Moses goes up on Mount Sinai, and for six days the mountain is covered with a cloud; then on the seventh day God speaks to Moses from the cloud. So "six days later" sets the background for divine/human communication. Jesus takes three disciples, Peter, James, and John, up the mountain, up a high mountain, the only high mountain in Mark. Galilee is not known for high mountains, but in Mark's story "high mountain" is probably more symbolic than geographical. It's a theological construct, a mountain where God and humanity come together (as I mentioned earlier with reference to Jesus' calling of the twelve on a mountain at 3:13). Jesus goes up there and is transfigured; he is changed; he appears as if from another realm. His clothes are so white that no bleach *on earth* could make them that white. The impression is unearthly; it's a quite different realm.

In addition, two other persons appear with him: Elijah—interestingly enough, mentioned first—representing the prophets; and Moses, representing the Law (or Teaching)—the two first and most important parts of the Jewish Scripture. Elijah and Moses are talking with Jesus. Then Peter, ever the one to hop in, says, "Well, uh, gosh, uh, let's, uh. Isn't it good we're here so we can, uh, do something? Let's, uh, let's build ... Let's build booths. Let's try to make this thing permanent. This is scary but exciting. I want this to last. Let's build something that will, uh, sort of freeze the moment." The narrator comments, "He did not know what to say, for they were terrified." He did speak up; you can't knock that. He did speak and he wanted to do something, but it was hard to know what to do in that circumstance.

Then a voice from the cloud—it never says God, but you'd have to be pretty slow not to get that—says, "This is my son, the beloved; listen to him." Suddenly the people who Peter was going to build the booths for aren't there any more, so it would have been rather useless. The audience is putting this all together; we think, "Okay, we've got the six days, we've got a mountain, we've got a cloud, we've got a voice; we've got a lot of Moses stuff going on here—a whole lot of Moses and God communicating. So that's the background." When we hear the voice saying, "This is my son," we remember the voice at Jesus' baptism, "You are my son," talking to Jesus. Now that the voice says, "This is my son," to whom is it talking? Well, Peter, James, and John, at the very least—not to mention maybe some other people out here in the audience too. We have also seen Peter struggle before, struggle to get it right. Peter "tracks down" Jesus. Peter is willing though not always able.

The audience has to be wondering, "Gosh, when God comes and says, 'Dah-tah-dah, listen to him,' you really want to know what Jesus is going to say next because that must be really important." Sure enough, coming down the mountain, Jesus says, "Tell no one what you've seen." And we think, "We've heard this one before. 'Tell no one what you've seen' is not exactly news." But, Jesus says, "Tell no one what you've seen *until*—until after the Son of Man has risen from the dead." For the first time we see—aha!—the messianic secret has an end. There comes a time when it's okay to say who Jesus is as Messiah; after the whole story is played out, then you can tell. So it does turn out to be a quite important thing that Jesus has to say.

The disciples are questioning among themselves what this "rising from the dead" could mean. Now they know what the term "resurrection" means because that's a first-century Jewish belief, especially among Pharisees, that at the end time there will be a resurrection. Some say everybody will be resurrected, then the righteous and unrighteous will be sorted out. Some say only the righteous will be resurrected; but it's a common enough belief, even though some (namely, the Sadducees) don't share it. What they really don't understand is exactly how this prediction relates to everything that is going on in their lives at the moment. So the disciples do something we frequently do: we want to ask a question about one thing, but we are chicken, so we ask a question about something related, hoping that answer will shed light. They say, "Why do the scribes say that Elijah must come first?" And Jesus says, "Oh, yeah. They say that. And he is coming first to restore all things." (This is Elijah who didn't die but was carried up into heaven in the chariot, so therefore is available to come back down and is going to come back down before the day of the Lord comes.) Then Jesus adds, "Elijah *has* come, and they did to him whatever they pleased, as it is written about him." The audience responds, "Right. We knew that. We knew that because, remember, when John came in the wilderness he dressed like Elijah, he ate locusts like Elijah, he said things like Elijah, so that's what this means: Elijah came in the person of John."

Exorcism and Prayer (Mark 9:14–29)

Jesus and the three get down the mountain, and they find a great crowd, some scribes, and the nine disciples. Apparently a man has come with a son who has an unclean spirit, and the father has asked the disciples to heal him. They have not been successful. The son has convulsions. Sometimes you hear about "the epileptic boy." The text doesn't say that, but that's a good description because he has convulsions and is thrown here and there. Jesus is discouraged; he says, "You faithless generation." Jesus doesn't blame the disciples; he doesn't blame the father; he doesn't blame the son. He just says in general, "You faithless generation, how much longer must I be among you?" Not "How much longer *can* . . . ?" but "How much longer *must* I be among you?" In other words, "How much longer must I put up with you? I'm on my way, down south, you know, to Jerusalem. And I'm feeling anxious about what's going to happen there, as I told you. So I'm trying to get you ready for me not to be here, and it's pretty discouraging."

When the spirit convulses the boy in the presence of Jesus, Jesus says, "How long . . . ?" It's very touching that Jesus, who is wondering how long he has to suffer with this faithless generation, asks the father, "How long have you suffered with this child being this way?" The father answers, "From his childhood. But if you are able to do anything, have pity on us." Jesus says, "*If! If* I'm able. All things can be done for the one who believes." Not *by* the one who believes, at this point, but *for* the one who believes. Immediately the man says, "I believe. Okay. If . . . if I need to believe, I believe." But he is sincere, and then he says, "Help my unbelief." This is a wonderful phrase because belief and unbelief are not polar opposites. This man is not two-sided. He knows that belief and unbelief come together. He says, "I believe; help my unbelief." Belief is always a process, never a state. This man embodies that. Jesus casts the spirit out of the boy, and the narrator says the boy was like a corpse. People think he's dead; Jesus lifts him up and he stands. Think about that. Bells ringing? Father, child, dead/almost dead, lifted up. Jairus and his daughter, right? Here we have another father—and a son.

Later, in the house, Jesus is talking to the disciples, and they are considerably worried: "Why couldn't we cast it out? Earlier [chapter 6] we cast out unclean spirits, but we couldn't cast this one out. We really are trying. What's our problem?" Jesus says, "Some can only be cast out by prayer. This was one of those really tough ones." Think about prayer. Jesus is preparing his disciples for his absence. One of the resources they will have in his absence is prayer. Think about Mark's audience. What resources are available to Mark's audience? Prayer is one of their resources too.

Second Passion Prediction (Mark 9:30–31)

Next Jesus is passing through Galilee, moving south. He started up in Caesarea Philippi, and he's come south. Unlike the material (Mark 4–8) we looked at in the previous chapter of this guide, here the material is quite directional: from the north to the south, on the way to Jerusalem. The narrator says, "He did not want anyone to know it; for he was teaching his disciples." And he was teaching them things like this: "The Son of Man is going to be betrayed, and he is going to be killed, and after the third day he is going to rise." Now we've heard that before—a passion prediction. We even know what might come next, and it does—a misunderstanding.

Misunderstanding (Mark 9:32–34)

The narrator says, "They did not understand what he was saying, but they were afraid to ask him." Yeah, right. As Ernest Best has said in *Following Jesus*, "their failure to understand is only partial: they understood enough to be afraid to ask to understand more." So they understood something. You know there are things in your life you don't want to understand too well. That's the way they were too.

Then they go into a house, by now a typical setting of Jesus and his community. At this point the house is in Capernaum; they are moving south, moving south. Jesus asks, "What were you talking about *on the way?*" They say, "Um. Um." They don't want to say anything because they were talking about who was going to be the greatest, and they sense that would probably not sit well with Jesus. But Jesus doesn't have to be told anyway.

Discipleship Instruction (Mark 9:35–37)

Jesus sits down, the authoritative position while teaching, and he calls the twelve—it's very solemn—and says, "Whoever wants to be first must be last of all and servant of all" (NRSV)—which is, of course, directed to their conversation. Then Jesus takes a child in his arms and says, "Whoever welcomes one such child in my name welcomes me, and whoever welcomes me welcomes not me but the one who sent me" (NRSV). Now children are not the picture of innocence in the first century. Sometimes in our society people think that, but those aren't parents, are they? In the ancient world, a child was mainly symbolic of powerlessness. Even a slave had some status as an adult, but children were the ones who got told what to do, where to go, when to talk, when not to talk—everything. They had little freedom to do anything. So a child is one who is *not* powerful. But Jesus presents children as images of the ones who enter the kingdom of God. How would a child enter the kingdom? Not gloriously. Not maneuvering to sit on one side or the other of the most important seat. So God is on the side of the powerless.

More Misunderstanding (Mark 9:38)

There follows *another* misunderstanding. (This is a very developed passion prediction unit here in the middle.) John informs Jesus, "We stopped someone who was casting out demons in your name because he wasn't following us"—not "he wasn't following *you,*" but "he wasn't following *us*"!

More Discipleship Instruction (Mark 9:39–49)

Jesus says, "Oh, don't do that—because whoever is not against us is for us. For truly I tell you, whoever gives you as much as a cup of water to drink because you bear the name of Christ—Christians, Christ-folk—will by no means lose the reward."

Then there are some more teachings and sayings; Mark has to fit the good stuff in somewhere. Several sayings have to do with the image of stumbling. "Whoever makes a little one stumble should have a millstone hung around his or her neck and be thrown into the sea." Well, you know where that would get you. "If your hand causes you to stumble, cut off your hand. Better to enter life without your hand than not to enter at all. If your foot causes you to stumble, cut off your foot. If your eye causes you to stumble, pluck it out." Now, literally, Jesus is not telling people to pluck out eyes and cut off body parts. This is hyperbole. Jewish storytellers do this all the time; good storytellers do this all the time. But it is saying, Take this seriously. Entering into the kingdom, or entering into life, is extremely important. This saying is followed by some even-more-miscellaneous metaphorical sayings about salt and fire, which explore how one can be preserved—that is, not spoiled—for the kingdom of God.

Reviewing Mark 9:30–50—Second Passion Prediction Unit

So what we have is a second passion prediction unit. Not only do we have a passion prediction, a misunderstanding, and discipleship instruction, but, just in case we didn't get it, we have another misunderstanding and further discipleship instruction. Don't feel badly about the disciples. Every time they don't understand, Mark gets to tell *you* again. And you are the important one here! The story is being told for the audience. It's not being told to characterize the disciples as this way or that way. It's being told to give the author, the evangelist, a way to communicate his good news to the audience. So every time the disciples need a little more instruction, you get some too.

THIRD LESSON (MARK 10:1–52)

We come, then, to a section of teaching. I read this chapter for years before I made any sense of it as a whole. It opens with a little geographical update: they're moving through Judea and beyond the Jordan. Oh, they're getting much farther south now. Galilee is in the north; and Samaria and Judea are further south. It was traditional for Jews to avoid going through Samaria because of the mutual disrespect of Jews and Samaritans going back to the fall of the northern kingdom in 722 B.C.E.

(Before the Common Era, or B.C., Before Christ). Travelers to Jerusalem would cross over to the other side of the Jordan and go south through the land "beyond the Jordan" to Judea. So we're definitely moving south, moving toward Jerusalem.

Teaching about Divorce (Mark 10:1–12)

Again crowds gather to Jesus; again he teaches them. Then some Pharisees come to ask Jesus a question "to test him": "Can people get divorced?" Jesus says, "Well, you're the Pharisees. You know the Law. What do you think? What does it say?" The Pharisees answer, "Moses said that men could write a certificate of dismissal and divorce their wives. Moses said that in the Law, according to Deuteronomy." Jesus responds, "Yes, that's true. Moses said that, but he only said that because of your hardness of heart. It's not the way it was supposed to be in the beginning. Look in the first book of the Law, in Genesis. There it says that God created them male and female, and a man shall leave his father and mother and go with his wife, and they shall be joined, and the two shall be one flesh. And one flesh should not be torn asunder. So in the beginning the intention was for marriage to be lasting; only for your hardness of heart did that other thing come up."

Then in the house the disciples ask about this teaching, and Jesus says, "Whoever divorces his wife and marries another commits adultery against her." Now you might hear this as if it were just the usual religious teaching. But this was quite radical. What does Jesus mean "commits adultery against *her*"? Everybody in the ancient Jewish world knows that adultery is an offense against a man. Adultery is an offense against the man whose wife is involved. If A and B over here are husband and wife, and C over there commits adultery with her, he commits an offense against A, her husband, the man. But Jesus says, "Oh, no. If you divorce your wife and marry another woman, you commit adultery against your first wife." Then Jesus follows up this radical idea with something equally preposterous: "And if she divorces her husband . . . " She divorces her husband? Not in Jewish Law, not in the ancient Jewish world. She doesn't divorce her husband; it's not an option. In the Roman world it was, yes; but in the world of Jesus, the Jewish world, she doesn't divorce her husband. In effect, Jesus is saying, "You know, I don't really like the way this world is going. I think I'll just turn it upside down."

So the status quo socially and religiously—religiously because this is in the Law—is being challenged. We have to consider, Who would have the most to lose in a divorce? It would be the woman because she would no longer have a home or a means of support. It's not as if she could go out and get a job! She leaves her father's home and goes into her husband's home; if she leaves her husband's home, she will not be welcomed back into her father's home. There's no place for her to go and no telling where she might be left. So restricting divorce is an attempt to protect the partners who are being most hurt by divorce—women.

Teaching about Children (Mark 10:13–16)

Next there's a teaching about children. The disciples, trying to be good, trying to do the right thing, are preventing people from bringing children to Jesus because he's got more important things to do. You know, he's the Messiah, and he's got things to tend to. So they tell people to keep the children out of the way. But Jesus says, "No, don't do that. It's to these children that the kingdom of God belongs. If you don't enter like a child—with some sort of humility and surprising gratitude— then you really won't enter at all." Remember that children embody not innocence but powerlessness; children are the ones in society who have the least protection and the fewest possibilities. Again the religious and social status quo is being challenged.

Teaching about Wealth (Mark 10:17–31)

The following teaching is about wealth. We're reminded again that we're "on the way." (Here the NRSV says "setting out on a journey.") A wealthy man questions Jesus about what must be done to inherit eternal life. Jesus says, "Okay, we'll start with the Ten Commandments," and he names off a few. Then the man says, "I've done all that—from my youth." Jesus says, "Very good. Nice start. Just one more thing, just one more thing to do: sell all that you have and give your money to the poor. Then you'll have treasure in heaven, and you can come follow me." Interestingly, the man never speaks again. He's just speechless. The narrator says he was shocked, and he went away grieving. He can't even say, "No. How could you . . . ?" or anything. He just . . . it's a truly sad moment.

The disciples are a bit surprised too because they think wealth is received from God and thus would be a blessing, so Jesus says to them, "How hard it will be for those who have wealth to enter the kingdom of God!" (NRSV). Then he gives us the wonderful hyperbole about the camel: "It's easier for a camel to get through the eye of a needle than for someone who is rich to enter into the kingdom of God." Now that's kind of amusing. But it's serious and difficult too. The disciples, perplexed and astounded, respond, "Well, gosh, can anybody be saved? How is anybody saved?" Jesus answers, "If it were just up to humans, nobody would be. Because for humans these things would probably not be possible. But, fortunately, it's up to God, and for God all things are possible." Peter pipes up and says, "Oh, we've left everything and followed you." Jesus says, "That's right, Peter, and you will be rewarded. There's no one who's left brothers or sisters or houses or fields or lands or whatever who won't receive a hundredfold in this life—with persecutions—and in the age to come eternal life. But many who are first will be last, and the last will be first." Lots of reversals of expectations going on here.

Reviewing Mark 10:1–31—Challenging the Status Quo

What we have then is a teaching about divorce that says men are not to be valued above women, a teaching about children that says adults are not to be valued above children, a teaching about wealth that says the rich are not to be valued above the poor. In Jesus' society, all of those formulations go the opposite way: the rich are more valuable, adults are more valuable, men are more valuable. And bang, bang, bang, three radical assertions in a row, and households are turned upside down. The household image, so important for early Christianity, is reversed, and the status quo is challenged.

Third Passion Prediction (Mark 10:32–34)

Then we get "on the way" again—this time quite explicitly: "on the way, going up to Jerusalem." The narrator says, "Jesus was walking ahead of them; they were amazed, and those who followed were afraid" (NRSV). Just walking down the road being amazed and afraid? Yes, because they are learning, and the people are beginning to pick up on this challenge to the status quo, and things are getting ominous. Jesus says one more time, "The Son of Man is going to be handed over to the chief priests and scribes, the Jewish leaders; and the Jewish leaders are going to condemn him to death; and then he's going to be handed over to the Gentile leaders; and they're going to do a whole bunch of things—mock him, spit upon him, flog him, kill him." Note the detail this time; it's almost a script of what comes next. "And then, after three days, he will rise." This is a passion prediction. What might you expect to happen next? Misunderstanding? Discipleship instruction?

Misunderstanding and Discipleship Instruction (Mark 10:35–40)

You're right; one, two, three. It's a technique ministers use in sermons too: first time, second time, third time. Teachers use it. And Mark is using it. James and John say, "We want you to do a favor for us." (Do your kids ever do this? They want you to do something for them and they don't tell you what it is. Always say "No.") Here James and John say, "We want to sit on your right hand and your left hand in your glory." Jesus says to them—rather politely, I think; I would have said "Glory? Who's been talking about glory?"—but Jesus says, "You don't know what you're asking. Can you drink the cup that I'm going to drink? Can you be baptized with the baptism with which I'm going to be baptized?" We know from early Christianity that these are images of suffering—drink the cup of suffering, be baptized in suffering; so that's very clear to the audience. Confidently James and John say, "We are able; we *are* able." Jesus does not deny their response but adds, "Well, you know what? You will. You will drink this cup and you will be baptized with this baptism. But, still, what you're asking is not mine to give; it's for those for whom it's been prepared, and I am not in charge. I've never said I was. I may be the anointed one, but I'm anointed by somebody else, and that somebody else is in charge of such arrangements."

Then the ten become angry at the two. The narrative doesn't say why. Do they become angry with the two because the two didn't understand about the suffering and the ten do? Or do they become angry with the two because some of the ten want to sit on the right and the left, and James and John asked first? It's not entirely clear. But Jesus talks to them all. He says, "All of you, all of you, listen up, not just you two. You know that among the Gentiles—Romans and the like—those whom they recognize as their rulers lord it over them. But it is not so among you; whoever wishes to become great among you must be your servant, for the Son of Man came not to be served but to serve. You can't buy into the power structures of the powerful." He's talking to a powerless group, and he says, "Don't replicate in your own midst the power structures of those who are oppressing you. Don't copy your oppressors. It's not really a good model." The final line is, "For the Son of Man came not to be served but to serve."

Reviewing Mark 10:32–45—Third Passion Prediction Unit

This is the final, the third and final, passion prediction unit: passion prediction, misunderstanding, discipleship instruction.

Healing a Blind Man (Mark 10:46–52)

The last story in this third major section of Mark begins: "And they came to Jericho." Remember the first story? "And they came to Bethsaida." The phrases are the same in Greek, except for the place names. Jericho is quite close to Jerusalem. At Jericho people try to prevent a blind man from coming to Jesus, rather than bringing a blind man to Jesus as at Bethsaida. But the blind man calls out loudly, "Jesus, Son of David, have mercy on me!" Finally Jesus hears him and calls him to come. There's a lot of calling going on here. When Bartimaeus and Jesus come together, Jesus asks, "What do you want me to do for you?" and Bartimaeus answers, "My teacher, let me see again." Immediately Jesus says—there are no verses I've left out—"Go; your faith has made you well." No saliva, no touching the eyes. The healings involving saliva happen in Gentile territory. Remember, in a Jewish world, saliva's not clean, so you don't want to heal Jews by that means. But "your faith has made you well"—does that ring a bell? Remember the woman who interrupted Jesus in the crowd and knew, even without talking to him, that if she touched even his garments she would be made well? Jesus had said to her, "Your faith has made you well." And he says to this man, "Your faith has made you well." And "immediately," the narrator says, "he regained his sight and followed him on the way."

So we have at 8:27, the beginning of the section, "on the way" to the villages of Caesarea Philippi, and at the very end of the section, 10:52, "on the way"—an obvious opening and closing. Remember, if you're a hearing audience, you're used to that. If you hear someone recite or retell the Gospel of Mark, he or she will probably accent certain phrases so that you will hear the echo of those phrases when they are said again later. Mark's Gospel seems ready and waiting for someone to say it in such a way that you hear something you couldn't see. Sometimes our ears are a better entrance into our minds than our eyes.

Where are we going on the way? The very next line, "When they were approaching Jerusalem . . . ," begins the final chapters of Mark's Gospel (11–16). By now it is clear that "on the way" is a metaphor for discipleship, for following Jesus. But where is Jesus going? He is moving from Galilee, where he has been a powerful teacher and healer, to Jerusalem, where he will end up suffering at the hands of the politically powerful. And "on the way" he has been teaching his disciples about a commitment to service so deep that it even involves being willing to suffer in the process of serving. Jesus is not going out of his way to get killed, but if that happens in the line of service, then it happens.

Reviewing Mark 8:22–10:52—Discipleship

If we look back at this whole section of the Gospel, we see a very strong framework.

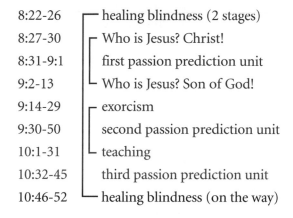

8:22-26	healing blindness (2 stages)
8:27-30	Who is Jesus? Christ!
8:31-9:1	first passion prediction unit
9:2-13	Who is Jesus? Son of God!
9:14-29	exorcism
9:30-50	second passion prediction unit
10:1-31	teaching
10:32-45	third passion prediction unit
10:46-52	healing blindness (on the way)

At the beginning there is a story of healing of blindness in two stages. At the end there is another story of healing of blindness and following on the way. After the first story we ask the question "Who is Jesus?" And Peter says, "The Christ." We know that's right because "Jesus Christ, the Son of God" is included in the title of the book. But does Peter understand it completely? Jesus wants to teach him more, so we have a first passion prediction. Peter misunderstands; Jesus gives instruction to Peter—and everybody around. Then the question is implicitly raised again, "Who is Jesus?" And God says, "My son." Again we know Jesus is the Son of God from the title of Mark: "The beginning of the gospel of Jesus Christ, the Son of God." That's another echo. Then when they come down from the Mount of Transfiguration where that voice is heard, they run into the problem with the exorcism, and the disciples say, "We could do this earlier, but we can't do this now." Jesus responds in effect, "Prayer, prayer, prayer. I can't be here forever. You're going to have to have some other resources. It's not like you're on your own, but you've got to open up the channels of communication."

Next there's a second passion prediction, with a misunderstanding, and more discipleship instruction—and some more misunderstanding and some more instruction—around the theme of not lording it over others and being the one to serve, not the one to be powerful. In the teaching section that follows, the status quo is turned on its head: Men are not valued over women, adults are not valued over children, the rich are not valued over the poor. In the first half of the Gospel we have exorcisms and teachings. Now we have one sample exorcism and one sample teaching. The teaching and the exorcism still go on, even when the service and the suffering come, but they are seen in a new framework. Finally there's the third passion prediction unit, with the detailed passion prediction, the misunderstanding again, and that final punch line of discipleship instruction: "The Son of Man came not to be served but to serve—to give his life as a ransom for many." Then the man is healed of his blindness and follows Jesus on the way—and, of course, that's the invitation to anyone who is hearing or reading the story.

We might ask then, what are Jesus' followers to understand—and to do—about the *kingdom,* the reign, of God that Jesus proclaims and brings (the focus of the first chapter of this guide)? And what are Jesus' followers to understand, and to do, about the *community* (second chapter focus) that Jesus gathers in recognition and anticipation of the kingdom? The community gathers in recognition of the kingdom's present reality, but in anticipation of its final fulfillment. The community is a continuing witness to that tension. What are Jesus' followers to understand, and to do, about the *discipleship* that following Jesus demands? If the lives of disciples are to reflect the pattern of their teacher's life, what does that mean for the followers of Jesus? This has been the focus of the present chapter and Mark's third major section.

My final point is to remind ourselves how different we are from Mark's first hearers. Mark's community was largely powerless. The first people who were attracted to the "good news" were people for whom it was really good news. Some were slaves; some were lower class people. It wasn't usually the rich and the powerful who were first attracted to the Jesus movement. Yet even those without power might wish to emulate the powerful, so it's still challenging to say, "You should not replicate the power structures of the powerful," even to those who have little chance to do so. It's one thing to say to people who have no power, "You are blessed because you have no power, and don't replicate among yourselves in small ways what the powerful do," but what does this mean for us?

Christian communities today frequently are the powerful. Some Christian churches are powerful groups. Some churches include powerful individuals. So what does discipleship demand in these cases? How is God's being on the side of the powerless good news to the powerful? This is good news to somebody, but is it good news to us? Is it good news to people who have power, and, if so, what is our discipleship call? If the people who have no power are not to replicate the ways of the powerful, what should the people who already have power be doing to be on the same side as God, to be thinking the things of God and not thinking human things (8:33)?

> *O God,*
> *whose way we, like Jesus, seek to follow,*
> *give us ears to hear the Gospel of Mark*
> *as good news of daring discipleship*
> *that manifests your love in startling ways*
> *in the world.*
> *Amen.*

Suffering

Mark 11:1–16:8

O God,
whom we, like Jesus, dare to call Father,
give us ears to hear the Gospel of Mark
as good news of your presence with us
through life and suffering and death
and beyond.
Amen.

Kingdom, community, discipleship, suffering—I have assigned these terms to four major sections of Mark's Gospel, although there is significant overlap. We considered community when we looked at kingdom; we considered discipleship when we looked at community, and suffering when we looked at discipleship. All these themes are interwoven, but the last chapters of Mark, 11 through 16, do focus on suffering.

As I mentioned in the previous chapter of this guide, we can divide the Gospel fairly evenly into two parts. The first part (chapters 1–8) has to do with the Jesus of power. Jesus is a powerful teacher; he's a powerful healer; he's got a powerful message: God is breaking into history. Yet the Markan Jesus says, "Don't tell; don't tell—because you only know part of the Jesus story if you know only that. You only know part of what it is to be a disciple if you know only that." So the second part of the Gospel (chapters 8–16) presents the Jesus of paradox. The "Jesus of suffering" would not be as appropriate a subtitle because the power doesn't exactly disappear; it seems to go underground. The power comes back in a different way. But the paradox is twofold: first, that someone who is so powerful does suffer, suffers at the hands of those who have political and religious power in his current society, and doesn't use the power he does have against the powerful; and, second, that somehow the suffering reveals the power.

The structure of this part of Mark is fairly simple; mostly this is the passion story, the story of Jesus' suffering and death. Probably the passion story is more familiar than anything else in the Gospel because of our celebrations during Lent and Easter. We usually hear this story in larger portions than we hear most of the other parts of the story. It is quite closely connected; it's more detailed than the rest of the Gospel. We hear about certain days and certain hours and certain places when and where things are happening, and we also hear more names of minor characters. Overall this is the story of the passion of Jesus. But the passion story seems split apart (chapters 11–12/chapters 14–16), and in the middle is placed the story of the passion of the community (chapter 13). This middle section, called the eschatological discourse (I will talk about that term later), declares that the community, the followers of Jesus, will suffer.

Mark 11–12   passion of Jesus (prelude)
Mark 13   passion of the community
Mark 14–16   passion of Jesus

So here's the story of Jesus' suffering—and not tacked on at the end as a postscript: oh, by the way, you're going to suffer too—but right in the middle of his own passion story Jesus says, "Aha, look at the future: You're going to go through this too. Take note and take heart."

The Longer Ending (Mark 16:9–20)

As part of this overview of the final section I want to discuss the longer ending of Mark, 16:9–20. I mention this passage now so I can set it aside because, like most scholars, I think it was added to the Gospel later. Textual scholars, who study the ancient manuscripts, conclude that the most trustworthy ancient manuscripts end at 16:8. After that, it's multiple choice, including a long ending and a short one. One manuscript has only the short ending; most have only the long ending. Some manuscripts have both the short ending and the long ending, and a few manuscripts insert some additional material in the middle of the long ending. All these endings have in common that they are static. Jesus sits—frozen and immobile—not doing a thing, but gloriously at the right hand of God. There's no more interaction, no more tension.

Indeed, it's the tension of Mark 16:1–8—with its ambiguity, fear, and uncertainty—that some people can't stand that led to these endings being written. Apparently, especially after Matthew and Luke were written with different endings, people read Mark and were unsatisfied with the ending, so they added on. If you want a longer ending, read Matthew or read Luke. Perfectly good endings for their Gospels. But the current ending that was added onto Mark on the basis of Matthew and Luke doesn't work nearly as well as the original endings of Mark, Matthew, or Luke!

So much for the longer ending of Mark. If you want to know more about the various Markan endings you can read about them in the footnotes of good study Bibles. I choose to mention the longer ending now because it is actually anticlimactic in relation to Mark's ending at 16:8, and I don't want to end later with an anticlimax. So here we will be looking at Mark 11:1–16:8—the passion of Jesus, or the prelude to it (chapters 11–12), the passion of the community (chapter 13), and the completion of the passion of Jesus (chapters 14–16).

THE PRELUDE TO THE PASSION OF JESUS (MARK 11–12)

The prelude to the passion of Jesus begins with the entry into Jerusalem. The narrator says Jesus and the disciples were going toward Jerusalem, and they reached Bethphage and Bethany at the Mount of Olives. These villages are within the environs of Jerusalem, parts of "greater Jerusalem" that during the Passover were technically inside Jerusalem. This arrangement was made to accommodate the crowds of people who came to Jerusalem for Passover; Jerusalem wasn't large enough to hold them, so the city limits were extended during Passover in order that all who came to the pilgrimage feast could meet the obligation to be in Jerusalem.

Entering Jerusalem (Mark 11:1–11)

Although this story is frequently called the Triumphal Entry, scholars don't usually call it that because it's not as triumphal as you might imagine. Jesus gives to his disciples an instruction that is a prediction: "You go into the city, and you find this colt, and you take the colt. . . ." And the disciples say, "Yeah, and we find people getting onto us too!" "And you tell them this," Jesus continues, "and they give you the colt." So they go and do exactly what he said, and exactly what he said happens. Now that's a minor part of the story, but it turns out to be important later on. Jesus predicts something, and what he predicts happens. So Jesus is riding a colt into Jerusalem, and he's getting a grand welcome—sort of a rolling out of the red carpet, except that it's provided by the people rather than by the officials. It is a way to show that he's an honored guest, that he is welcome. The people sing out, "Hosanna!/ Blessed is the one who comes in/the name of the Lord!/Blessed is the coming kingdom/of our ancestor David!" (NRSV). Jesus' coming indicates the beginning of the rule of God, which some in the crowd connect to the tradition of David's kingdom.

Then there's a charming verse some scholars call "Jesus as tourist": "Then he entered Jerusalem and went into the temple; and when he had looked around at everything, as it was already late, he went out to Bethany with the twelve" (NRSV). You know, he got there on a tour bus, he went in and saw everything—kind of once over; he was tired, so he went back to his hotel, had the buffet supper, and went to bed early. The question is, Why did he go in and go out? The answer probably has to do with what the author wants to do next. Mark is juxtaposing Jerusalem with its temple and Bethany with the twelve. Jesus is setting up an alternative space, an alternative center of power. His center of power is not the temple; he is not a priest; he is not powerful in the sense that he has authority over others given by the temple. So the Jerusalem temple is the seat of one type of authority, and over against it stand Bethany and the Mount of Olives.

Cursing a Fig Tree (Mark 11:12–14)

The next morning, Jesus goes from Bethany to Jerusalem, and on the way he sees a fig tree. I remember as a teenager being very upset about this story. Jesus sees a fig tree, and he goes over to see if it has any figs; when it doesn't have any figs, he curses it. That's bad enough, but then the narrator says, "It didn't have any figs because it wasn't the season for figs!" As a teenager I thought, "Boy, if I did that my dad would really be angry with me." Cursing a tree that doesn't have fruit in the season when it doesn't bear fruit? Now if I had gone out into a citrus grove my father cared for or owned in the middle of August, and looked for fruit, and then cursed a tree because it had no fruit, that would be ridiculous because summer is not the season for citrus fruit. Something strange is clearly going on in Mark's Gospel. I tell my students, "If the text makes no sense literally, that's a cue that it's probably not meant to be taken literally. Maybe it's telling you you're on the wrong wavelength."

So, we take a second look at the word "season." The word is *kairos*. *Kairos* is one Greek word for time; *chronos* is another one. *Chronos* indicates one thing, another thing, another thing. *Kairos*, on the other hand, means the right moment. Jesus' first words in Mark's Gospel are "The *kairos* is fulfilled; the right moment has come." It's a quality of time. We know that some time is better than other time, right? Some time is more meaningful. *Kairos* is meaningful, fulfilled time. The story may still not make a whole lot of sense, but we're getting closer to understanding it.

Clearing the Temple (Mark 11:15–19)

Then Jesus goes right into Jerusalem and into the temple, and he casts out the sellers and the buyers. How many of you were taught that he casts them out because they were crooked and were charging too much money? Did anybody ever hear that explanation besides me? The text simply doesn't say that. If the problem had been unscrupulous merchants, the Markan Jesus would have cast out just the sellers, not the buyers also, since they weren't doing anything wrong. Yet Jesus casts out the buyers and the sellers, all the money changers and all the people who were in the temple to do the very thing the temple was built to do—offer sacrifice as a symbol of devotion to God. This observation is extremely important. If you don't have money changers, you can't buy a thing. You can't take Roman coins with their pagan images into the temple, so you have to have money changers. If you don't have animals to buy for the sacrifice, people can't offer the appropriate sacrifices. You can't take your lamb all the way from Nazareth to Jerusalem! By the time you get there the poor thing would be worn out, and it has to be a perfect lamb. So unless people can buy and sell in the temple, the temple can't work. And that's what seems to be happening. The temple is being cleared out—not cleansed, not prepared so that it will be better, but closed down.

Jesus says, quoting Scripture, "My house should be a house of prayer for all nations, and you have made it a den of robbers." You might think, "Ah, robbers! See, they *were* crooked." But think that through. Where do robbers steal? Do they steal in their own den? Well, if there's no honor among thieves, maybe they do. But they generally steal from others; then they take the goods into their den. The den of robbers is the protected place where the thieves get together in safety to divide up the booty they got elsewhere. Their den is not where they commit the crime. Thus the image suggests that something is wrong outside the temple, and the temple is the place used to bless and protect the wrongdoing. We have to watch out and read the words that are actually there.

Withered Fig Tree and Prayer (Mark 11:20–25)

I still haven't said much about that fig tree! Jesus goes back home, that is, to Bethany (11:19). The next day he comes in, and the fig tree is withered—and the disciples are amazed. Jesus, not so amazed, says, "When you pray for something, you must trust that your prayer will be effective. You must trust God to hear your prayer; you must trust there will be some result from prayer, that it's not just exercising your tongue. And if you do that, then amazing things will happen." And, while he's on the subject of prayer, Jesus adds, "Another thing important about prayer is forgiveness: If you forgive others, then you'll be forgiven of your own sins in your prayer to God, but not otherwise."

Reviewing Mark 11:12–25—The Time for Prayer

Here we have a Markan sandwich: something about the fig tree, something about the temple, and then something about the fig tree again. A-B-A. Mark presents this sequence so that the inside can interpret the outside and the outside can interpret the inside. We know that, in the ancient world, temples and trees were often connected—a holy tree, a holy place. Here the fig tree serves as an image of the temple of Israel. It's not the time for the temple any more; therefore the temple can be shut down. When would Mark's audience hear this story? Probably just after the destruction of the temple. The destruction of the Jewish temple was a catastrophic event for Jews *and* for early believers in the Christ, both Jewish and Gentile. Imagine hearing, in the wake of this catastrophe, "But Jesus anticipated that the temple would be shut down. And he said it would be okay because the temple is supposed to be a house of prayer for all nations. Can we pray without a temple? Yes. Can we offer sacrifices without a temple? No. So only the sacrifices are really lost, and sacrifices are definitely less important than prayer. The sacrifices were specifically Jewish, prescribed by Jewish Law. But prayer is for all nations, Jews and Gentiles." In the first century this complex story would have been comforting. For us it's at first mystifying, but it would have been comforting to people of the time who were questioning whether God had abandoned the people of God. The answer of Mark's Jesus is a reassuring, "No. God has come near. You can live without the temple; you can't live without prayer."

Previewing Mark 11:27–12:44—Teaching in the Temple

Then Jesus goes into the temple; the narrator particularly states that he is walking in the temple. He doesn't sit down because that's the authoritative position of the teacher while teaching, and the temple is not the seat of Jesus' authority. While he's there, different groups of Jewish authority figures come before him, one group at a time, and ask him a question. They want to try to trick him, but in each case the tables are turned and he tricks them instead.

By Whose Authority? (Mark 11:27–33)

The chief priests, scribes, and elders ask, "Where do you get your authority to do these things?" Which things? Maybe the throwing out of the buyers and sellers, maybe his whole ministry. Jesus responds, "Okay, I'll answer your question, if you'll answer mine. Where did John get his authority to baptize?" They think this through: "Well, if we say John got his authority from God, then Jesus will say, 'Why didn't you follow him?' So we won't say that. If we say, 'He got his authority from human beings,' then all these crowds who follow John and were baptized by him are really going to riot. And we don't want that either. So we'll just say, 'We don't know; we can't say.'" And Jesus says, "Okay, then I won't answer your question either." Jesus, one; religious authorities, zero.

Parable of the Vineyard (Mark 12:1–12)

Then Jesus tells a parable against *them,* and at the end of the parable the narrator says, "They knew that he told the parable against them." They got it; they got it all right. Jesus says, "There was an owner who planted a vineyard, and he took very good care of the vineyard." Everybody from the chief priests to Mark's audience knows that Israel was God's vineyard. But the tenants, those caring for the vineyard on behalf of its owner, fail to give the owner his share of the fruit at the harvest time. They mistreat the owner's messengers and even kill his son, thinking to take over the vineyard themselves. And the chief priests, scribes, and elders understood that he told the parable against them. They are supposed to be taking care of the vineyard, and Jesus is saying, "You're not doing a very good job; you're just about to get kicked out."

Taxes to the Emperor? (Mark 12:13–17)

Then the Pharisees and the Herodians are sent to test him. They ask, "Should we pay taxes to the emperor?" Jesus sees it is a trap. If he says "Yes," then they will say, "Oh, listen, crowd, he said we should pay taxes to Rome. Do you like that attitude in your Messiah?" If he says "No," they will say, "Oh, Roman guard, Roman guard, did you hear this? He's telling people not to pay their taxes." Either way he loses. So Jesus says, "Well, bring me a coin." Where are they at the time he says that? Somewhere in the temple! Jesus doesn't happen to have a pagan coin on him in the temple where it's not allowed, but they seem to! So they produce the pagan coin, and Jesus looks at it and asks, "Whose picture is that?

Whose name is that? Oh, the emperor's? Well, then give it back. Give back to the emperor what belongs to the emperor in the first place, *and* give to God what belongs to God." That's pretty open-ended; he doesn't specify exactly what belongs to God, but the Pharisees and Herodians are silenced. Jesus, two; religious authorities, zero.

Questioning Resurrection (Mark 12:18–27)

The Sadducees come and say, "*We* can trick him. We're going to ask him a question about the resurrection because we don't believe in the resurrection, and he does and the Pharisees do. But we know there's no such thing as resurrection because it's not mentioned in the first five books of the Law, the *real* Scripture." So they say, "A man with seven brothers was married, and he didn't have any children, and he died. The Law (in Leviticus) says that his brother should marry his wife and raise a child in his name. So the first brother married her, but he too died. That happened with brother two also, and brother three married her and died, and brother four, and so on." No one worries about the poor woman— having to be first wife and then widow of all those brothers! Finally even she dies. Then the Sadducees cast the hook, "In heaven, whose wife is she going to be?"

Jesus says something like, "Who told you that in heaven the patriarchal rules of marriage will apply? I mean, who told you that? You think God in heaven is going to follow the patriarchal rules you've made up about marriage and about women belonging to men and all that kind of thing? I really doubt it. In heaven everyone will be like angels; nobody will belong to anybody. Everybody will be free. So forget it, and besides, have you never read the Law . . . ?" Imagine, saying to the Sadducees, "Have you never read the Law?"! "In the Law," Jesus points out, "in the second book of the Law, in the passage about the bush, we read that God says to Moses, 'I am the God of Abraham, and Isaac, and Jacob.' I *am* the God, not I was. If God still *is* the God of our ancestors, then our ancestors are not dead—otherwise God would have had to use the past tense. If they're not dead, even though they lived long ago, then they must be resurrected." Now that grammatical argument may sound a little picky, but it is good rabbinical argumentation; it's a good first- and second-century rabbinical argument. So the Sadducees lose. Jesus, three; religious authorities, zero.

An Exceptional Scribe (Mark 12:28–34)

Then just about the time you're thinking, "Any Jewish authority is going to lose," one comes who doesn't. A scribe comes to Jesus, but he doesn't come to test him. He asks, "What is the greatest commandment?" And they agree; Jesus and the scribe agree that the greatest commandment is to love God above all. Jesus adds, "And the second one—you didn't ask, but I'll just mention it anyway—is to love your neighbor." The scribe responds, "Yes, that's right." Finally Jesus says to him, "You are not far from the kingdom of God." Don't underestimate this wonderful little story. Just about the time you think Mark's Gospel is completely stereotypical in its characterizations—all Jewish leaders are bad—the stereotype does not hold. There's a little wedge, and it pries open our thinking. After that, no one dared to ask Jesus another question.

Other Scribes (Mark 12:35–40)

Jesus himself says a few things. First *he* asks a question, "Why do the scribes say that the Messiah is David's son?" The Markan Jesus' argument runs something like this: David is the speaker in Psalm 110, and there he says, "The Lord said to my Lord," which means "God said to the Messiah." So David calls the Messiah "my Lord," and you certainly don't call your son "my Lord." Thus how could the Messiah be David's son? This exchange can be confusing to us because later Christian tradition does affirm that in some way the Messiah is the son of David. But Mark seems to present a different angle on this subject. Then Jesus says, in general, "Beware of the scribes. They like attention wherever they go (marketplaces, synagogues, banquets), and they rob widows of their inheritances."

A Poor Widow (Mark 12:41–44)

Then, almost immediately, a widow shows up. Jesus notices her, in the temple, giving two coins, two tiny coins, into the treasury. Jesus says to his disciples, "Look at her. She's giving more than everybody else. What she's giving is her whole life." The translations tend to lead you astray here; they usually say she gives "her whole living," keeping you on the literal economic level. Mark's Gospel opens up another dimension in her giving of "her whole life," her whole *bios*. She is not an example for a stewardship campaign. (I hate it when she is cast in that role.) She is more than that; she is a model for what Jesus is in the process of doing—giving his whole life—and for what disciples must be prepared to do. For that reason Jesus calls his disciples' attention to her, and then departs the temple.

Reviewing Mark 11:27–12:44—Controversy in the Temple

The story of the poor widow closes a series of controversy stories between Jesus and the religious authorities. Does that sound familiar? There was a series of five controversy stories back in 2:1–3:6. Jesus got into trouble, and he got into trouble, and he got into trouble . . . usually by doing something on the Sabbath, not just by talking. The earlier controversy stories developed primarily from Jesus' actions as a healer, but also as one who called sinners. The later controversy stories develop primarily from Jesus' actions as a teacher. In the first set the religious authorities involved are scribes and Pharisees. In the second set the key religious authorities are temple officials: chief priests, scribes, and elders. The first set concludes with the comment that the Pharisees and Herodians sought a way to destroy Jesus. The second set foreshadows the success of the temple authorities in turning him over to the Roman authorities for execution. The story of the poor widow who "gives her whole life" closes not only the second series of controversy stories but also the entire subsection, the prelude to the passion of Jesus.

THE PASSION OF THE COMMUNITY (MARK 13)

We move now to the passion of the community or what is more generally called the eschatological discourse. This long word, eschatological, comes from two Greek words: *eschaton,* meaning "the last things," the end time, and *logos,* meaning "teaching about." Eschatology has to do with thinking about the end time, understanding what's going to happen at the end of history.

Destruction of the Temple (Mark 13:1–3)

The setting is quite important: they come *out* of the temple, and as they are coming out, a disciple says, "Wow! Look at those large stones! Aren't they magnificent?" Perhaps you have been to Jerusalem and seen the Western Wall. If so, you know "large" doesn't do these stones justice. They're humongous; they're the size of a room in a house today. So I can understand the disciple's point of view. However, Jesus says, "Not one stone will be left on a stone; I'm unimpressed." If Mark's story were told in 70 of the Common Era, just after the temple destruction, wouldn't it be comforting to know that this catastrophe was bound to happen? Wouldn't it be reassuring to know that Jesus had not only predicted it but had given clues for how to survive the loss of the temple?

Political and Natural Disasters (Mark 13:4–8)

Jesus now sits; he sits on the Mount of Olives. Now he's in his own place, opposite the temple. The narrator stresses this location: "opposite the temple." There Jesus is particularly talking to four: Peter, Andrew, James, and John. When Jesus talks to three or four, it's a special event, but we're always invited. The disciples say, "What will be the sign of this? When is this going to happen—this thing about the stones?" Basically Jesus is a scholar at this point; rather than giving them a straightforward answer, he says, "Well, let me tell you the negatives." You ask a scholar to give you a definition, and she says, "Let me tell you what it's not." So Jesus says, "Let me tell you when the end is not. Don't be led astray. Some people will say, 'I am he. I am he; the culmination of the end is happening right now.' There'll be war; there'll be rumors of war; you'll be told, 'The end is now; the end is now.' No, the end is still to come. Earthquakes. Famines. 'The end is now; the end is now.' No, this is just the beginning of the birth pangs. There are going to be political disasters; there are going to be natural disasters. There always have been, and they are going to continue some more. So just because you have political and natural disasters doesn't mean the end is here yet."

Challenges for Followers (Mark 13:9–13)

Jesus continues, "Hang on. In the future you are going to be persecuted. *You* are going to be handed over to councils [that's Jewish councils] and beaten in synagogues; the religious authorities are going to persecute you. You'll stand before governors and kings for my sake; the political authorities will persecute you. But the good news must first be preached to all nations. That might take a while. The good news has to get out to everyone, so persecution is going to happen. When you're brought before these councils, when you're brought before the governors and kings, don't worry about what you're going to say. The Holy Spirit will speak, not you; it will speak right through you; you just have to be present and not be too afraid. Families will be split, brothers and children. There are going to be all sorts of traumas within the community as well as from outside. But the one who endures to the end will be saved. I'm not promising you it will be easy; it is going to be tough, but don't lose hope."

Apocalyptic Events (Mark 13:14–23)

Then we read some traditional material from apocalyptic Judaism. "Apocalyptic" comes from a word that means "revealed." The last book in the Bible is called the Apocalypse, or Revelation, the revealing of what's to happen at the end time. In Mark, Jesus quotes something from Daniel, saying, "But when you see the desolating sacrilege set up where it ought not be (let the reader understand) . . ." (NRSV). And I only wish I could! I only wish I really knew what was so obvious to the first Markan audience that the author could simply allude to it obliquely. Scholars have all sorts of theories, of course, but we don't really know. Something dramatic happened. The phrase about the "desolating sacrilege" in Daniel seems to be a cryptic allusion to the actions of the Greek ruler Antiochus Epiphanes. When it's ripped out of Daniel and put into Mark it's even more cryptic. Perhaps it refers somehow to the temple destruction by the Roman rulers, which is more than but at least "a desolating sacrilege." Apocalyptic material is always quoting previous apocalyptic material. So Mark quotes Daniel, and Revelation quotes Daniel, and materials get recycled.

When Jesus says, "For in those days there will be suffering, such as has not been from the beginning of the creation that God created until now, no, and never will be" (NRSV), that is standard apocalyptic. Apocalyptic always views the present time as the worst it's ever been. It couldn't possibly be worse than this, could it? We happen to live at the very worst moment of history. Right? Have you ever heard that? This is a recurrent theme of apocalyptic. "False messiahs will come. False prophets will come. But be alert; be awake; be watchful. I've already told you everything." Think of how comforting that must be: When all of these things are beginning to happen, you can say, "Oh, yes, we knew this would happen; it's okay; we were expecting this." When I was going through childbirth I remember thinking, "I'm sure glad I attended childbirth classes and knew this was going to happen. This experience would be even harder to take as a total surprise." It's the same feeling with the crises of the end time. If you're going through these crises, it's good to have been warned.

Cosmic Events (Mark 13:24–27)

Then we have the cosmic aspects—all traditional material from apocalyptic Judaism. The sun, the moon, and the stars will all fail. The sun and moon are supposed to give light, but they will fail to do so. The stars are supposed to stay fixed so that the people out on boats can know where they're going, but the stars will start moving. Then, quoting Daniel again, the Son of Man will come on the clouds. Plus there's this wonderful addition to the quotation from Daniel: "The Son of Man will send out angels, or messengers, to gather the elect from the ends of the earth to the ends of heaven." Two clichés have come together. There's one cliché that says "from one end of the earth to the other," and another that says "from one end of heaven to the other." The Markan version is broader than either: "from the ends of the earth to the ends of heaven." Everybody will be gathered together. That's comforting too, isn't it? All the elect will be found, wherever they are—and included in the culmination of God's reign.

Parable of the Fig Tree (Mark 13:28–31)

We move to a parable of a fig tree. (We've heard a fig tree story before.) This one says, "When you see the leaves coming out on the fig tree, you know that summer is near, so when you see these things taking place, you'll know that 'it' is near or 'he' is near [you can't tell which in Greek], at the very gates. Truly I tell you, this generation will not pass away until all these things have taken place." Very apocalyptic: we live at that worst time, so this is going to happen in our lifetimes. "Heaven and earth will pass away, but my words will not pass away" (NRSV).

God Only Knows (Mark 13:32–33)

However, juxtaposed with these apocalyptic predictions is something even stranger. Jesus has just been declaring, "You can't believe it when people say, 'It's happening here,' but I can tell you that this will happen first, and this will also happen." So you feel you have some clues about the end time. Then he adds, "But about that day or hour no one knows, neither the angels in heaven, nor the Son [which would be me], but only the Father" (NRSV). Do you feel this rug coming out from under you? Whoa. Jesus is the one who's just been saying, "This will warn you, and that will warn you." Then he says, "Oh, by the way, did I forget to tell you? I don't really know. I don't really know when it's going to happen. Only God knows when it's going to happen." So the moral of that story is "Beware; keep alert; for you do not know when the time will come." A whole chapter on when and how the time is going to come concludes, "But don't take this too literally because you don't know when it's going to come. I don't even know when it's going to come." The point of all that is that you have to live your life prepared for the end to come—even if you don't know exactly when it's coming. Mark's Jesus would be dismayed at those today who try to calculate the coming of the end time by applying apocalyptic imagery to current events rather than focusing on living lives prepared for whatever end God has in mind whenever.

Parable of the Doorkeeper (Mark 13:34–37)

The parable of the doorkeeper illustrates this point. A man goes on a journey; he puts the doorkeeper in charge. The doorkeeper has to open the door when his master comes back, but he doesn't know when his master is coming back. But the doorkeeper better be there when "the lord of the house" returns. Do you get it? Where does Jesus meet with his disciples? In the house. Who is "the lord of the house"? Jesus. You don't know when "the lord of the house" will return, but you'd better be ready when he does. And the way to do that is to be ready at all times. The last line of the chapter is "And what I say to you—you four—I say to all. . . ." Well, how many is all? The other eight? Or those who do the will of God? Or the community who's hearing this? Or whoever reads it? It's a broad statement: "What I say to these, I say to all. I say watch, be alert, be awake." Don't calculate the time that God only knows; live in mindfulness of a future beyond human knowing. That's a fitting close to the subsection, the eschatological discourse or the passion of the community.

THE PASSION OF JESUS (MARK 14–16)

This section moves back to the passion of Jesus: the trial, the crucifixion, the resurrection. A very specific time is mentioned: two days before the Passover and the Feast of Unleavened Bread.

Plot against Jesus (Mark 14:1–12)

The chief priests would have many things to do at that time, but they've added a new item to their agenda: They're looking for a way to kill Jesus.

They don't think they can pull it off during the feast because of the crowds that follow Jesus. They'd like to do it as soon as possible, though they might have to delay. It's a very unholy action to be planning at that holy time of the year. At the very time in which they are supposed to be following the prescriptions of the Law for Passover, they are conspiring to bend the Law in removing Jesus.

A Woman's Anointing (Mark 14:3–9)

Jesus and his disciples are in a different place; they're in a house—the house of Simon the Leper in Bethany. Now maybe Simon is healed; maybe Jesus healed him, but it doesn't say that. So it may even be an "unclean" place. While they're at the house of Simon the Leper at table, a woman whose name is not given comes in and anoints Jesus' head with precious ointment. This action makes him "the anointed one," in Greek, *Christos;* in Hebrew, *Messiah.* The narrator doesn't actually say in the text, "That makes him the anointed one." All along, the author has been expecting the audience to make such inferences. There's a bit of an argument about whether the money she used for the ointment would have been better used for the poor. But Jesus says, "You can always help the poor—and you should. You won't always be able to help me, as she has done. She has anointed my body beforehand for burial." There's some connection between the Messiah and burial. That's an unusual connection: Messiah and death and burial. Then Jesus says to his followers, "Her story will be proclaimed in the whole world, wherever the gospel is preached, in remembrance of her." And, you know, it's true. Her story is so proclaimed. But without her name— perhaps her name is everywoman.

Judas's Betrayal (Mark 14:10–11)

Then the narrator says, "Judas Iscariot, who was one of the twelve [in case you forgot], went to the chief priests in order to betray" Jesus. There's a dramatic pattern to the way Judas is named in Mark's story. When his name is first mentioned in chapter 3, when he is called as one of the twelve, the narrator says, "Judas Iscariot, who betrayed him." So this action comes as no surprise. The other times Judas is mentioned all occur in the passion story, and every time he's men- tioned the narrator says, "Judas, one of the twelve." It's ironic; it's painful. The chief priests promise to give Judas money. There's a kind of irony here too: the woman gives up money for Jesus, and we don't even know her name; but Judas, one of the twelve, gives up Jesus for money. A sad reversal.

We can see other reversals here as well. Not only do we have Judas and the woman in opposite positions, but we also have the planning committees doing different things. The planning committee of the chief priests, scribes, and elders is planning a death. The planning committee of Jesus and the disciples is planning a celebration of Passover.

Observing the Passover (Mark 14:12–25)

On the first day of Unleavened Bread—wow, all that took place in one day—when the Passover lamb is sacrificed, Jesus says to the disciples, "You've got to go find a room for our Passover observance." The disciples ask, "Well, how do we find a room? It's so crowded in Jerusalem." Jesus answers, "Oh, you go, and you find this man carrying a jar of water [which is a little unusual, since mostly women do that], and you say this, and you do that." They go; they find the man carrying water; they say this, and they do that. And exactly what he predicts happens. The audience remembers that in chapter 13 Jesus predicted a lot of things to happen. What's the probability of those predictions being right? Is this a guy with a good record of predictions? Well, he predicted the finding of the colt, and that happened; he predicted the finding of the room, and that happened. So our confidence is building that what he said about his followers getting turned over to authorities will also happen. Then he predicts, in that room with the twelve, that one of his disciples will betray him. Now we know that's going to happen because we've already seen the preview. So his batting average is a thousand.

At this last meal, a Passover meal, we hear the set of four verbs that we've heard before: Jesus takes the bread and he blesses the bread and he breaks the bread and he gives the bread. Do you remember when you heard that before in Mark's Gospel? Twice. At the feeding of the five thousand, he takes and blesses and breaks and gives. At the feeding of the four thousand, he takes and blesses and breaks and gives. We know that these stories were used in the early Christian church as emblems of the Eucharist, as symbols of Communion, the Lord's Supper. Jesus says, "This bread is my body." Of course, bread and wine would have been at the table for Passover because they're symbolic foods for Passover. He says, "This [cup of wine] is my blood of the covenant, which is poured out for many. Truly I tell you, I will never again drink of the fruit of the vine until that day when I drink it new in the kingdom of God" (NRSV).

Do you ever think of this when you celebrate Communion—or the Eucharist, or Mass, or whatever it is called in your church community? The Markan Jesus says, "I won't drink it again with you until that day when I drink it new in the kingdom of God," and yet, in ways that you can't really explain and can't really deny, you know that Jesus is with you in that experience. So what does that tell you about that experience? And what does that tell you about the kingdom of God? The kingdom of God is indeed breaking into history, and at that moment of communion you are receiving a foretaste of the kingdom of God.

Predicting Peter's Denial (Mark 14:26–31)

After they had sung the hymn, which was the conclusion to the Passover ritual, they went out to the Mount of Olives, which is opposite the temple—as you remember from before. And Jesus, quoting Zechariah, says, "'The shepherd will be struck and the sheep will be scattered.' But after I am raised up [which is not the first time he's mentioned that], I will go before you to Galilee—where we all live." Then, in case you don't get the metaphor about the shepherd, Jesus says, a little more explicitly, "You will all desert me. Peter will deny me." Peter says, "No, not me— maybe them, but not me." And they all say the same. It isn't just Peter. They all say, "No. How could we possibly do that?" But how good has Jesus been at predicting? Pretty good, one hundred percent!

Praying at Gethsemane (Mark 14:32–42)

So Jesus goes out to a place called Gethsemane, which seems to be on the Mount of Olives, and takes with him three disciples—it's going to be a special moment—Peter, James, and John. He says, "All I want you to do is stay awake with me. I'm going to be in prayer; I'm sad and I'm worried, so I need some support." He prays, "Abba, Father, for you all things are possible [which he had said earlier with reference to entering the kingdom of God]. Remove this cup from me [The cup is an image of suffering used earlier with reference to James and John.]. Yet, not what I want, but what you want." Jesus does not have a martyr complex. He's not out to get himself killed. His anguished thinking goes something like this: "God, have you thought of a way to save me? Have you thought of a plan B? You know, plan A is looking really bad, and I wouldn't mind an alternative. But, if you can't think of one . . . I'm willing to go through with it."

Jesus comes back to the disciples, his moral support group—and they're sound asleep. "Try. Try to stay awake with me," he pleads. "And this time stay awake and pray." He goes away, prays the same words to God again, and returns to find them sleeping again. Even a third time, the narrator tells us, he goes away and prays and returns to find them sleeping. The image is clear: Jesus is praying/they're sleeping, Jesus is praying/they're sleeping, Jesus is praying/they're sleeping. We wonder if this is the prelude to how well his followers are going to do when times are tougher! We know it's looking discouraging. The third time Jesus says, "Enough. The hour has come."

Betrayal, Arrest, Desertion (Mark 14:43–52)

And at that moment Judas comes, one of the twelve, with a crowd bearing clubs and swords from the chief priests, scribes, and elders. The sign of betrayal they had agreed upon was a kiss. How ironic, how sad. Not only is Judas one of the twelve, but a kiss, a mark of friendship, is the mark of betrayal. Jesus is arrested. In the fray, someone cuts off the ear of the slave of the high priest; nothing more is told about it in this Gospel, but the Gospels of Luke and John add details. Jesus asks, "Do you have to come out with swords and clubs? I was with you in the temple every day teaching, and you didn't touch me then. Why not? Why now? But let the Scripture be fulfilled."

Then they all desert; they all desert, as Jesus had predicted. A most curious story follows. One more person we didn't even know was there deserts. A certain young man was following him—"following" is a discipleship word—wearing nothing but a linen cloth. The guards catch hold of him, but he leaves the linen cloth and runs off naked. They had grabbed the cloth, but it wasn't regular clothes, so he just ran out of it and into the night. Some would say, "Ah, this is an allusion to the author." The story is unique to Mark's Gospel, and who else would have known about this but the author John Mark himself? Well, since I think the Gospel is anonymous, I probably don't think it's an allusion to the actual author, right? In fact, I think it's an allusion to the audience!

In the ancient world a linen cloth might be used as a summer nightgown, a shroud for the dead, or a garment for those newly baptized in Christ. The linen cloth of the young man in 14:51 might allude to any or all of the three. He enters the story at night, when a nightgown might be worn—usually, of course, in one's house. The Greek word for linen cloth, literally just linen, *sindon*, occurs in Mark only here at 14:51 (twice) and at 15:46 (twice), where it refers to the linen cloth bought by

Joseph of Arimathea and wrapped around Jesus' body before laying him in a tomb. The term "young man" *(neaniskos)* also occurs in only two places in Mark: here at 14:51 and at 16:5, where a young man (dressed in a white robe, not a linen cloth) tells the women that Jesus is not in the tomb but has been raised. Desertion as a disciple, death, resurrection. The mysterious young man who runs away naked seems symbolically connected to all three. And, like the woman who gives "her whole life" and the woman who anoints Jesus "beforehand for burial," this young man remains nameless.

Death and resurrection are also associated in baptism, a third occasion for wearing a linen cloth. As Paul wrote in his letter to the Romans some years before Mark's Gospel, "Do you not know that all of us who have been baptized into Christ Jesus were baptized into his death? Therefore we have been buried with him by baptism into death, so that, just as Christ was raised from the dead by the glory of the Father, so we too might walk in newness of life" (Romans 6:3–4). Early believers were baptized in the nude—although our evidence for this dates from some years after Mark's Gospel. In their newness of life, the baptized returned to the state of Adam and Eve before the Fall: "naked and unashamed" (Genesis 2:25). The baptized go back to being Adam and Eve with all those possibilities; then they receive a new garment, a white linen cloth. Some scholars argue that Mark's Gospel was told in its entirety at baptismal services—to those waiting with linen robes. Even if this was not its setting—and more strongly if it was—this curious story of the follower who leaves his linen cloth and runs away seems to be a way of asking, "Were you there when they arrested our Lord? Did you run away, you who say you are going to be faithful followers? Are you always going to be faithful? You might as well know when you're baptized that you're probably going to fail sometimes. You're not going to make it all the time, and that's part of being baptized too. And that's part of being a follower too. Discipleship is a death and resurrection experience." This is a possible reading of a dramatic little story the author seems to think needs no further explanation for the audience.

Before the Council (Mark 14:53–65)

Then Jesus is brought before the Jewish council, at the high priest's house. Peter is in the courtyard of the high priest's house. There's false testimony. They say, "He said this"; they say, "He said that." They don't agree. Jesus mostly doesn't say anything. Finally the high priest says, "You've got to say something. Are you the Christ? Are you the Son of the Blessed One [that is, God]?" So Jesus responds, "I am, but I really don't want to talk about the Christ. It's a title everybody else uses, but I like to talk about the Son of Man. And you will see the Son of Man seated at the right hand of Power." The title "Christ" occurs occasionally—and significantly—in Mark, as does the title "Son of God." But they never occur on Jesus' lips. From Jesus' lips we hear about the Son of Man, the person who judges with God's authority at the end time. As his death approaches, Jesus does respond to the high priest's direct question with "I am," although it seems more like "Okay. All right already. I accept it, but . . ." Then Jesus deflects attention to the coming of the Son of Man in judgment.

Jesus is condemned to death for his presumed blasphemy. Some people blindfold him and strike him, saying, "Who hit you? Who hit you? You're a prophet; you should be able to predict who's going to hit you. Who did hit you?"

Peter's Denial (Mark 14:66–72)

At the same moment some people are teasing Jesus as a "prophet," his prediction of Peter's denial is coming true. Jesus is in the high priest's house; Peter is below in the courtyard. Jesus says, "I am" to the high priest, thereby assuring his death. Peter says, "I am not" to the high priest's servant girl and to the bystanders to escape his possible death, thereby fulfilling Jesus' prediction. At the very moment they're saying, "Prophesy! Prophesy!" the prophecy is coming true. Peter denies Jesus thrice; the cock crows twice; and Peter weeps. Short, but not sweet.

Before Pilate (Mark 15:1–15)

Then Jesus is turned over by the Jewish council to the Roman authority, Pilate, the governor. Pilate asks, "Are you the King of the Jews?" "King" is the term a governor would use; it has clear political implications. Jesus answers, again begrudgingly, "You say so. It's not the way I would talk about myself or my role." But mostly Jesus is silent, and Pilate is amazed because all these things are being said about him and he's hardly saying anything at all. Pilate doesn't think Jesus should be killed, and he discovers a way to get out of it by invoking a tradition that the governor should release one person at the festival of Passover. We have no knowledge of any such tradition outside the Gospels. Roman historians don't say anything about it at all, but it's part of Mark's plot. Pilate seems to be hoping, "Maybe they'll choose Jesus, and then I can let him go." But they don't choose Jesus; they choose Barabbas. Barabbas is an Aramaic name meaning, literally, "Son of the Father." Talk about irony! Instead of choosing Jesus to be let go, they choose the Son of the Father. Instead of the Son of the Father, they choose the Son of the Father. "And what shall I do with Jesus?" asks Pilate. The crowd cries out, "Crucify him!" "Why? What evil has he done?" Pilate answers back. But in the end, Pilate, wishing to satisfy the crowd—not a very heroic Roman posture—releases Barabbas and hands Jesus over to be flogged and then crucified.

As we hear the passion story of Mark's Gospel, where the story of Jesus' conflict with the religious authorities of his own Jewish community comes to its climax, we must remind ourselves of some of our original assumptions about Mark's Gospel. It was written long ago, far away, and from faith to faith. To hold twentieth- and twenty-first-century Jews responsible for actions reported in a passionate but one-sided story told for early believers in the Christ concerning first-century Judeans is morally reprehensible—as history has sadly shown. Such anachronistic blaming is as ridiculous as holding contemporary Italians responsible for Jesus' crucifixion by the Romans! Mark's Gospel is careful to portray the conflict as a conflict *within* the Jewish community and Jesus' death as the result of Roman imperial *power*. We must not miss the implications of these narrative facts for our own situations by transforming the conflict to "Judaism" versus "Christianity." We must have ears to hear the story as told.

Crucifixion (Mark 15:16–32)

In Mark's story, before Jesus is crucified by the Romans he is humiliated in other ways. In the ancient world it was not assumed that authorities would try to treat a criminal humanely. Here the authorities are making fun of Jesus, putting a purple robe on him. "Oh, you're the king! We'll put a crown on you—a crown of thorns." They continue with spitting and mocking, to humiliate him—and to warn any others who might follow his lead. This is how the powerful can treat the powerless when the powerless—even though they're powerless—threaten the powerful. Jesus is perceived as a threat. You don't get crucified for petty larceny. You get crucified for threats against the established government, threats against Rome.

Apparently they flog him a bit too much because he isn't quite able to carry the cross, that is, the crossbeam that would be placed on the vertical stake at the crucifixion site. Usually the prisoner would carry it himself, but Simon of Cyrene, which is in North Africa, is compelled to carry the cross for Jesus. He carries it to the place of the skull, Golgotha—possibly so called because the hill was in the shape of a skull. Jesus is offered wine mixed with myrrh—presumably to reduce the pain, but the narrator says he doesn't take it. They crucify him at about nine o'clock in the morning, that is, during the third Roman watch. They divide his clothes. The condemned are crucified naked; that is part of the humiliation. On the cross his offense is inscribed: "The King of the Jews." This indicates a political offense: He said *he* was the King of the Jews instead of the one appointed by Rome. He is crucified between two insurrectionists or outlaws—a more accurate translation than "bandits"—two people who really were trying to challenge the Roman overlordship.

Everybody mocks him. Passersby deride him. The chief priests and scribes mock him. Those crucified with him taunt him. The chief priests and scribes say, "Let the Christ, the King of Israel, come down from the cross now, so that we may see and believe." The audience has got to think, "Ah, see and believe—they're such important phrases in Mark. You know, you can sometimes see and not see. You can see people and they look like trees walking, and then you can really see. And when you really see, then what do you do? You follow Jesus on the way." The characters mocking Jesus on the cross are taking "see and believe" so literally. The audience has learned that seeing and believing are much more serious than that.

Jesus' Death (Mark 15:33–41)

There's a darkness over the whole land, which means, of course, that the sun must be failing to give its light—an expected feature of the time of apocalyptic judgment. The time is fulfilled. Jesus cries out, "My God, my God, why have you forsaken me?"—first in Aramaic, then in Greek, in the story told in Greek. We know these words are the beginning of Psalm 22, a prayer central to early believers' struggles to make sense of the horror of the crucifixion. Read Psalm 22; it starts out with this cry of forsakenness, but that's not where it ends up. What we don't know is whether we are to imagine Jesus just saying the first lines but thinking all the way to the end. Does Mark portray Jesus as moving through this lament—opening with, "God, why have you have forsaken me?" but closing with the psalmist, "I know you'll come back to me, and when you come back to me I will proclaim your name everywhere" (author's paraphrase). We don't know; here he just says the first line. We really don't know. Some characters think he's calling Elijah because the "Eloi" ("my God" in Aramaic) sounds like "Elijah" to them. "Maybe he's calling Elijah," they think. "Maybe he'll be rescued. Maybe he doesn't have to do this." But he does. There is a loud cry, and he breathes his last.

At that moment two dramatic events occur. The curtain of the temple is torn in two, from top to bottom. This curtain probably separates the Holy of Holies from the rest of the temple; thus it separates where the presence of God is most manifest to the high priest in the temple from the place where all the rest of the people can be. Even the high priest can go into the Holy of Holies only once a year. So what does it signify when the curtain is torn down? Where's God? Exploded outward! Boundaries that were separating the secular and the profane, God and humanity, are broken through. Then the centurion, the Roman guard, says, "Surely this man was God's son. Surely this man was Son of God." We recognize this designation from the title in 1:1, but the centurion at the cross is the only human character in all of Mark's Gospel who says that Jesus is Son of God. The demons know it. The unclean spirits know it. But no human knows it until the cross— because, in Mark's theology, only at the cross can we see what it means to be Son of God. Remember, "son" is one who is obedient. Son of God does not refer to Jesus' divinity; his sonship refers to his obedience, his obedience to God. When we see Jesus' death, as the centurion does, then we know more than the half-truth. Then we can tell, as the centurion does. It is, of course, ironic that it is a Roman centurion who first makes this human confession of Jesus as Son of God. But Mark's Gospel, and especially its passion narrative, is no stranger to irony.

The audience might well ask, "Where are the disciples?" When John was killed by a political authority (Herod), his disciples came and took his body and laid it in a tomb. And where are Jesus' disciples now? The narrator seems to say, "I thought you might ask about that. There are women—men were expected? There are no men—but there are women looking on from a distance. They used to follow him and minister to him (serve him, "deacon" him) when he was in Galilee. And there were also many other women who had come up with him to Jerusalem." ("Follow" and "serve" are discipleship words.) The final word of Jesus' discipleship instruction following the third and final passion prediction is "For the Son of Man came not to be served but to serve" (10:45, NRSV). Yet only angels (1:13) and women (1:31; 15:41) are reported to serve in Mark's narrative. It's almost as if the narrator is saying to the audience, "If you were imagining Jesus in Galilee with only men as disciples, you have to rewrite your whole story. You have to go back and reimagine that all over again because there were women there all the time. Gotcha! I wasn't mentioning them by name because I am a first-century writer after all, but, now, surprise of surprises, it is the women who are there at the end—the ones we least expected. They are the ones who serve. They are there as his followers at the very end."

Jesus' Burial (Mark 15:42–47)

It was evening; it was the Day of Preparation, that is, the Day of Preparation for the Sabbath. It would be inappropriate for the Jews to carry out the burial rites for the body on the Sabbath. So Joseph of Arimathea, who's Jewish, comes and asks for the body. Not only is Joseph Jewish, he's a Jewish leader. He's "a respected member of the council" of the chief priests, scribes, and elders, which decided to turn Jesus over to Pilate, who decided to crucify him. Are all of the chief priests, scribes, and elders opponents of Jesus? Not quite—here's Joseph of Arimathea. Are all the religious leaders in the temple opponents of Jesus? Not quite—remember the scribe not far from the kingdom of God? Are all the synagogue leaders opponents of Jesus? Not quite—remember Jairus? Jairus, one of the scribes, Joseph of Arimathea—there's always a wedge in Mark. It's not easy to get away with stereotyping in Mark's story; there's always a break. (Let anyone with ears to hear, hear.) The narrator says Joseph is looking for the kingdom of God. He asks Pilate for the body of Jesus. First Pilate makes sure he's really dead. He's really dead. Then Joseph gets the body, wraps it in a linen cloth, and lays it in a tomb—like the disciples of John did for him. Joseph of Arimathea is not one of the twelve; neither are the women at the cross. Yet they are followers.

At the Tomb (Mark 16:1–8)

Two women see where the body is laid (15:47). They want to do the women's work, which is to anoint the body with oil and spices, but they don't have the spices in hand, and they can't buy them because it's the eve of the Sabbath. So when the Sabbath is over, as early as they can the next morning, they go to the market to get the spices and then to the tomb to anoint the body. They're a little worried about the stone that sealed the tomb because it was really big. But when they get there the stone has been rolled away; the door is open, and a young man—it doesn't say an angel; it just says a "young man" clothed in a white robe—is sitting there. (It is easy to be reminded of the "young man" who ran away naked, leaving his linen cloth, as he, along with Peter and the other disciples, deserted Jesus at his arrest.) The young man at the tomb says to the women followers, "Oh, you're looking for Jesus of Nazareth. He's not here. He has risen, as he told you. But go and tell his disciples, especially Peter, that he is going ahead of you to Galilee. There you will see him, just as he told you." So the women flee, but the narrator adds, "They said nothing to anyone, for they were afraid." And that's the last word; that's the last word of the Gospel. "They said nothing to no one, for they were afraid." In Greek the double negative shows intensification. This is a very strange ending—full of tension.

Now ask yourself, where is Jesus in this picture? He's not in the tomb. He's not in the clouds. (That's the picture of the later and longer ending, 16:9–20.) Where is he? He's said to be going ahead to Galilee. He's on the way; he's in process; he's in movement. He's going home; he's going where the disciples are going to go. They're certainly not going to stay in Jerusalem where it's dangerous; they're going back to Galilee to try to put their lives back together. And when they get there, when they get back to their old lives, they'll find out their journey wasn't useless; it isn't hopeless—and it isn't over! They'll find that Jesus has come to Galilee ahead of them.

The disciples—women and men—returning home will know that Jesus has come to comfort them, to strengthen them for continued proclamation of the *kingdom* of God, the growth of the community, the development of *discipleship*—and the possibility of *suffering*. Kingdom, community, discipleship, suffering. Here at the end we seem to be beginning over. The audience realizes that Jesus' death is not the end—that is the meaning of resurrection. Jesus' death is not the end of the coming kingdom of God, not the end of the community of discipleship—probably not the end of the suffering either because Jesus said that in the future his followers too are going to suffer.

For Mark's community, a powerless and possibly persecuted group, discipleship seems to have entailed actual suffering at the hands of the powerful. Mark's Gospel suggests that such persons should put their own suffering in the context of Jesus' suffering at the hands of the religiously and politically powerful. This view gives hope of God's enduring presence and new life. Think of it this way: Put your suffering, first-century community, in the middle of the story of Jesus' suffering and see if that doesn't give you a new perspective on it. Suffering is not the end. Even death is not the end.

For Mark's community, suffering was a real experience. Christian communities in Europe and North America today are frequently powerful and rarely persecuted groups. Yet there are Christians in some places in South America, Africa, and Asia who are being persecuted for their faith; perhaps they are in solidarity with some of Mark's first audience. But many of us are not suffering for our faith. In addition, sometimes our own power entails the suffering of others. So Mark's story puts us in a bit of a bind. We need to ask ourselves, What are the dangers when the good news told to the powerless is taken over and proclaimed by the powerful? Can this good news both comfort the afflicted, as it was meant to do in the first place, and afflict the comfortable, which it probably needs to do for us today? Can the good news of God's presence in the world be heard by all of us—powerful as well as powerless? Can it be told by all of us? And how do the powerful need to hear things and tell things differently from the powerless?

The final line of Mark's Gospel is that the women at the empty tomb "said nothing to no one." But did you hear the story? Well, then they must have said something to someone at some point! The audience must ask why the author would stop the story at this moment—with the followers' fear and silence. Perhaps because that's the moment of highest tension. Were you there? Were you ever afraid? Were you ever afraid to tell the story? Were you ever afraid to share the good news? Then you know what it's like to be caught up in that moment. Will you tell the story now? Will you live the story now? The title of Mark's Gospel is "The *beginning* of the good news of Jesus Christ, the Son of God"—not the ending. The good news is that even death is not the ending of the good news. So the whole story is just the beginning. Like Jesus at the close of Mark's Gospel, we're always "on the way."

> *O God,*
> *whom we, like Jesus, dare to call Father,*
> *give us ears to hear the Gospel of Mark*
> *as good news of your presence with us*
> *through life and suffering and death*
> *and beyond.*
> *Amen.*

❖ ❖ ❖

Echoes

Mark 1:1–4:34	**Kingdom**
Mark 4:35–8:26	Community
Mark 8:22–10:52	Discipleship
Mark 11:1–16:8	Suffering

We've learned that Mark's Gospel is self-titled: "The beginning of the good news of Jesus Christ, the Son of God." In chapters 1 through 4 we heard how Jesus was called "son" by God at his baptism. Jesus would be obedient to God. We saw Jesus' obedience in his proclamation of the coming of the kingdom of God, that is, God's coming near to rule the earth. The in-breaking of the kingdom was manifested in Jesus' powerful teaching and in his powerful healing and exorcising. The kingdom demands community—not only the twelve disciples, but "whoever does the will of God." Could that be us?

> *O God,*
> *that we like Jesus might be called*
> *your sons and daughters,*
> *give us ears to hear the Gospel of Mark*
> *as good news of your kingdom*
> *breaking into the world through our lives.*
> *Amen.*

Mark 1:1–4:34	Kingdom
Mark 4:35–8:26	**Community**
Mark 8:22–10:52	Discipleship
Mark 11:1–16:8	Suffering

In chapters 4 through 8 we heard how the community of those who do the will of God was stretched to include not only Jews, the ancient people of God, but also Gentiles. The Sea of Galilee, a political boundary between Jewish and Gentile territories and a natural challenge for the disciples, becomes for the Markan Jesus a bridge uniting those on both sides. On both sides of the Sea, Jesus teaches, heals, and feeds the people—both Jews (his own people) and Gentiles (those beyond his group). Can his followers be led to this new level of sight and insight in understanding their role in proclaiming the kingdom of God? Can we?

> *O God,*
> *that we, like Jesus, might be brothers and sisters*
> *with all your people,*
> *give us ears to hear the Gospel of Mark*
> *as good news for an inclusive community*
> *beyond the boundaries that restrict our love.*
> *Amen.*

Mark 1:1–4:34   Kingdom
Mark 4:35–8:26   Community
Mark 8:22–10:52   Discipleship
Mark 11:1–16:8   Suffering

In chapters 8 through 10 we heard the struggles of Jesus to explain and of the disciples to understand his way of service rather than domination. Three times Jesus predicts that his way will lead to suffering; three times the disciples show their preference for power. Three times the audience listens in on their discipleship instruction. As the characters in the story move along the way to Jerusalem, the audience moves with them in understanding the way of discipleship as a way that challenges the religious and political status quo when that status quo values men over women, adults over children, the rich over the poor, us over them, and power over service. Do the disciples move from seeing Jesus as the Christ like "trees walking" to the clear sight of Bartimaeus who follows Jesus on the way? Do we?

> *O God,*
> *whose way we, like Jesus, seek to follow,*
> *give us ears to hear the Gospel of Mark*
> *as good news of daring discipleship*
> *that manifests your love in startling ways*
> *in the world.*
> *Amen.*

Mark 1:1–4:34   Kingdom
Mark 4:35–8:26   Community
Mark 8:22–10:52   Discipleship
Mark 11:1–16:8   Suffering

In chapters 11 through 16 we heard how the radical teaching of Jesus—with its challenges to the religious and political status quo—eventually entailed his suffering at the hands of the religiously and politically powerful. In the middle of the story of Jesus' passion, we heard also a hint of the story of the community's passion. The future of the Markan Jesus was the present of the Markan community. Placing their own suffering in the context of the story of Jesus' suffering offered hope of the continuing presence of God—through suffering, through death, and beyond. Mark's Gospel comes full circle. Only at its ending do we understand its beginning: This *whole* story is the *beginning* of the good news of Jesus Christ, the Son of God. That is the good news: The story of the in-breaking of God's kingdom or reign in the world did not end with Jesus' death. Death is not the end. Death is part of the story of the continuing presence of God with us. That part of the story we call resurrection, and Mark's Gospel is wise to be shy in trying to describe it further. But Mark's Gospel clearly suggests that resurrection means that what seems to be the ending might well be the beginning.

> *O God,*
> *whom we, like Jesus, dare to call Father,*
> *give us ears to hear the Gospel of Mark*
> *as good news of your presence with us*
> *through life and suffering and death*
> *and beyond.*
> *Amen.*

Extras

This book has presented an overview of Mark's Gospel, a listener's guide for those who seek to hear this good news more perceptively and more powerfully. If your appetite is more whetted than satisfied, I am pleased indeed! Offered here are some suggested starting places for your next engagement, whether further study of commentaries on Mark or listening to the Gospel presented orally. Resources are listed in two categories: If you want to learn more about Mark's Gospel and If you want to listen to Mark's Gospel.

IF YOU WANT TO LEARN MORE ABOUT MARK'S GOSPEL

If You Want to Learn More about Mark's Gospel as Story

Malbon, Elizabeth Struthers. "Narrative Criticism: How Does the Story Mean?" Pages 23–49 in *Mark and Method: New Approaches in Biblical Studies.* Edited by Janice Capel Anderson and Stephen D. Moore. Minneapolis: Fortress Press, 1992. Also included as chapter 1 in Malbon, *In the Company of Jesus* (see listing below).

Provides a brief introduction to "narrative criticism" (the scholarly study of the Gospels as story), including discussion of its roots in the New Criticism and structuralism; the narrative elements of implied author and implied reader, characters, settings, plot, and rhetoric; an application of narrative criticism to Mark 4:1–8:26; and suggestions for further reading.

————. *Narrative Space and Mythic Meaning in Mark.* Sheffield, England: Sheffield Academic Press, 1991.

————. "Echoes and Foreshadowings in Mark 4–8: Reading and Rereading." *Journal of Biblical Literature* 112 (1993): 213–32.

————. *In the Company of Jesus: Characters in Mark's Gospel.* Louisville: Westminster John Knox Press, 2000.

The preceding three works present the more complete arguments and scholarly references that lie behind the current work—the first exploring spatial settings, the second the characters around Jesus, and the third aspects of the rhetoric of Mark 4–8.

Rhoads, David, Joanna Dewey, and Donald Michie. *Mark as Story: An Introduction to the Narrative of a Gospel.* 2d ed. Minneapolis: Fortress Press, 1999. Web site: http://www.philologos.org/guide/books/rhoads. david.1.htm.

Provides an outstanding, fuller treatment of narrative critical analysis of Mark's Gospel, including separate chapters on the narrator, settings, plot, characters (two chapters, one focusing on Jesus), and the reader, with discussions of rhetoric intertwined. After an introductory chapter the book opens with a fresh translation of the Gospel of Mark, designed (without chapter and verse markings) to be inviting to read as the story it is. The main body of the book is complemented by an afterword on "Reading as a Dialogue: The Ethics of Reading."

If You Want to Learn More about Mark's Gospel and Oral Tradition

Bryan, Christopher. "Was Mark Written to Be Read Aloud?" Part 2 of *A Preface to Mark: Notes on the Gospel in its Literary and Cultural Settings.* New York: Oxford University Press, 1993.

Presents a fuller discussion of oral composition and transmission and an examination of oral characteristics of Mark's style. (Part 1 of Bryan's book asks, "What Kind of Text Is Mark?"—the question of genre or literary type.)

Dewey, Joanna. "Oral Methods of Structuring Narrative in Mark." *Interpretation* 53 (1989): 32–44.

———. "From Storytelling to Written Text: The Loss of Early Christian Women's Voices." *Biblical Theology Bulletin* 26 (1996): 71–78.

Both of these articles offer engaging discussions of the oral context into which Mark's Gospel came and the impact of that context on the way Mark's story unfolds.

If You Want to Learn More about Mark's Gospel through Exercises and Discussion

Malbon, Elizabeth Struthers. Online study guide for *Hearing Mark:* www.trinitypressintl.com.

Suggests individual and group exercises created to be used in conjunction with this guide in order to enhance understanding and appreciation of Mark's Gospel when read or heard.

Rhoads, David, Joanna Dewey, and Donald Michie. *Mark as Story* (listed above).

Includes two helpful appendices, one providing exercises for an overall literary analysis of Mark, the other exercises for a narrative analysis of episodes.

IF YOU WANT TO LISTEN TO MARK'S GOSPEL

If You Want to Listen to (and View) Mark's Gospel on Videotape

McLean, Max. *Mark's Gospel as told by Max McLean.* 101 min. Available from Fellowship for the Performing Arts, P.O. Box 230, Convent Station, NJ 07961-0230; phone for ordering: 1-888-876-5661; phone: 973-984-3400; fax: 973-898-1690; e-mail: info@bibleonstage.org; Web address: http://www.bibleonstage.org/ or http://www.listeners bible.com. Videocassette.

Presents the Gospel of Mark in its entirety, based on the New International Version, a translation not often used by scholars but frequently preferred by conservative Christian groups. Max McLean, with postgraduate training in acting and some seminary training, has been presenting the Scriptures professionally to a range of audiences since 1983. The presentation was recorded live before a studio audience, whose faces are shown only occasionally, whose laughter is heard gently in the background, and whose applause is heard and seen at the end. McLean wears contemporary casual clothes (shirt and slacks) and uses minimal props (a chair and a low wall); likewise, the production aspects of the videotape are unassuming but effective. McLean presents the entire Gospel from memory—with both authority and humor. His voice inflections, facial expressions, and body movements invite the hearer/viewer to enter into the story world. The presentation style involves a distinctive pattern of enunciation and speech rhythms; some listeners/viewers may find the portions of rapid speech challenging; others will likely find the alternation of fast and slow recitation dramatically effective. There is a brief pause after Mark 9:1, and a title screen ("Act II") appears before 9:2; this has the effect of ending Act I with a statement about "power" and beginning Act II with a manifestation of power and authority, the transfiguration. McLean closes with the longer ending of Mark, 16:9–20, which, on the basis of strong textual evidence, most scholars believe to have been added to Mark's Gospel later.

Rhoads, David R. *Dramatic Presentation of the Gospel of Mark.* 112 min. Available from SELECT, 2199 East Main Street, Columbus, OH 43209-2234; phone: 614-235-4136, ext. 4021; fax: 614-238-0263; e-mail: select@trinity.capital.edu; Web address: http://www.elca.org/dm/select/order.asp?sort=Title. Videocassette.

Presents the Gospel of Mark in its entirety, using the performer's own (quite literal and forceful) translation (also given in *Mark as Story,* listed above). Dr. Rhoads is a Markan scholar and a professor at Lutheran School of Theology at Chicago. The performance was recorded in a studio; in the absence of a live audience, the performer addresses directly the camera and thus the audience viewing the videotape. Dr. Rhoads wears a simple costume (brown robe and sandals) and uses minimal props (three white "cubes" as seats in front of a stage curtain); likewise the production aspects of the videotape are unassuming. The strength of the presentation lies in the simple but powerful telling of the story. Rhoads presents the entire Gospel from memory—with clarity, humor, and wonder. His voice inflections, facial expressions, and body movements—taking on each individual character—invite the hearer/viewer to imagine what it was like to be in Mark's first-century audience. A title frame after 8:21 ("You don't understand yet?") marks the "End of Part I," and "Part II" opens with 8:22, the healing of the blind man at Bethsaida; this has the effect of ending Part I with a question directed first to the disciples then to the audience and beginning Part II with a break in the text often recognized by New Testament scholars as significant.

————. *Dramatic Presentations from the New Testament.* Available from SELECT, 2199 East Main Street, Columbus, OH 43209-2234; phone: 614-235-4136, ext. 4021; fax: 614-238-0263; e-mail: select@trinity.capital.edu; Web address: http://www.elca.org/dm/select/order.asp?sort=Title. Videocassette.

Offers dramatic presentations of five selections from the New Testament, along with a brief and helpful commentary introducing each one. Here Dr. Rhoads presents Mark 8:22–10:52, the "way" section of Mark's Gospel (27 min.). The commentary is informative and engaging; the presentation style is the same as that described above.

(The other New Testament selections presented are from Galatians [30 min.], Matthew [21 min.], Luke [14 min.], and John [24 min.].)

Runyeon, Frank. *AFRAID! The Gospel of Mark.* 52 min. Available from Runyeon Productions, P.O. Box 6393, Thousand Oaks, CA 91359; phone: 800-984-8472; e-mail: FrankRunyeon@aol.com. Videocassette. Offers selections from the Gospel, chosen, translated, and woven together by the performer, who might be known to some viewers as "Steve Andropoulos" of the daytime TV show *As the World Turns.* Although a professional actor, Runyeon has had theological training as well, earning a degree in religion from Princeton University and a Masters of Arts degree from General Theological Seminary in New York. The presentation was recorded live on Good Friday, 1997, before a church audience, members of whom Runyeon approaches occasionally as if they were other characters in the story. The laughter of the audience is heard gently in the background. Runyeon wears contemporary casual clothes (white pullover shirt and slacks) and uses minimal props (candles, a tall stool, a stand on the altar). However, other production aspects are more elaborate: Lighting includes candlelight and a series of spotlights in different places in the sanctuary (to which Runyeon moves with urgency and drama), including aisles as well as the chancel area; intriguing original music by Paul Avgerinos overlays the presentation. Runyeon presents selections from the Gospel from memory—with both drama and humor. His dramatic (even melodramatic) voice inflections, facial expressions, and body movements invite the hearer/viewer to respond to the characters. Title frames divide the presentation into Act One—The Secret (chapters 1–5), Act Two (chapters 6–13), Act Three (chapters 14–16). The presentation of the Markan story is framed by a direct address to the audience. The introductory address sets the scene as a secret meeting of Christians hiding in the catacombs in Rome to avoid persecution by Nero who has been blamed for the fire in Rome. (While the reference to Nero's blaming of Christians comes from the Roman historian Tacitus, historians are aware that the catacombs were not used as hiding places for Christians but as burial places.) Runyeon represents "Mark" telling the story to keep it alive. After 16:8 (which he presents as the end of the Gospel, following the scholarly consensus), Runyeon adds an epilogue challenging the audience to go and tell the story, announcing that "The Gospel begins here." Because the performance is a synopsis, the hearer/viewer will not be able to pick up all the patterns suggested in this book, but the performance itself is powerful.

If You Want to Listen to (and View) Mark's Gospel in Live Performance

Dewey, Dennis. *Jesus Christ, the Son of God: Stories from Mark's Gospel.* 90 min. Dennis Dewey, who calls himself a minister of biblical story, has performed and led storytelling seminars all over the United States and Canada as well as in Europe, New Zealand, Australia, Korea and Israel. Ordained as a minister of the Presbyterian Church (USA), he has been engaged full time in this itinerant, ecumenical ministry of biblical story since 1992. Because this presentation is of selections from Mark's Gospel rather than the entire Gospel, the audience will not be able to pick up all the patterns suggested in this guide, but the performance itself is powerful. Dewey also leads workshops, retreats, and tours focused on biblical storytelling. Dennis Dewey may be reached by mail at 107 Ridge Road, Utica, NY 13501; phone: 1-800-STORY-XL (USA) or 1-315-797-1163 (international); fax: 1-315-797-2951; e-mail: DenDew@aol.com; Web address: http://www.dennisdewey.org/.

McLean, Max. *Mark's Gospel.* (See the description of his videocassette above.) Other selections from the Bible are also available. Max McLean may be reached by mail at Fellowship for the Performing Arts, P.O. Box 230, Convent Station, NJ 07961-0230; phone: 1-888-876-5661; e-mail: info@bibleonstage.org. Information about his performance schedule and booking are available on the Web at http://www.bibleonstage.org/ or http://www.listenersbible.com.

Network of Biblical Storytellers (NOBS). A national group of persons (scholars, students, laity, clergy) dedicated to furthering the art of biblical storytelling. The group may be able to put you in touch with a storyteller near to where you live—or help you become that biblical storyteller! For information, you may contact the headquarters of NOBS by mail at United Theological Seminary, 1810 Harvard Boulevard, Dayton, OH 45406; phone: 1-800-355-NOBS or 937-278-5127; fax: 937-279-0848; or e-mail: nobsint@nobs.org; web address: http://www.nobs.org/.

Runyeon, Frank. *AFRAID!* Professional performances of a synopsis of Mark's Gospel. (See the description of his videocassette above.) Runyeon may be reached by mail at Frank Runyeon Productions, P.O. Box 6393, Thousand Oaks, CA 91359; phone: 800-984-8472; e-mail: FrankRunyeon@aol.com; Web address: http://newlifeseries.org/Bios/Runyeon.html.

Viewing and listening to a video performance of the Gospel of Mark can be an ear- and eye-opening experience, especially when prepared for by study of the Gospel. Watching and listening to a live performance of Mark's Gospel (or selections from it) can be even more moving. Both experiences can also be challenging and even frustrating. To tell a story is to interpret a story. You may not even be aware that you have your own interpretation of Mark until you hear someone else telling it in a way that sounds strange to you. Some listeners find some strong presenters overwhelming because they seem to leave so little room for differing interpretations within the audience. If this is ever your experience, feel good that you are aware of the inevitability of interpretation—yours and that of others. Rejoice that you are so deeply engaged with the story. But listen now, and later speak what you hear.

If You Want to Listen to and Participate in a Group Reading of Mark's Gospel

I offer these suggestions based on about a decade of experience of my local church (Christ Episcopal Church, Blacksburg, Virginia) with hearing the four Gospels—although we began with Mark! Like this listener's guide, these suggestions are offered for your own appropriation and adaptation to your situation.

BEFORE THE READING

1. Solicit readers, ideally from among those who have been engaged in a study of Mark's Gospel, for which a group reading will be a culminating experience. Don't overlook young people as readers. (Remember what the Markan Jesus says about children!) Their interpretive voices often help adults hear anew.

2. Select a translation that all will use. I highly recommend the New Revised Standard Version. Using a variety of translations is helpful at the study phase but distracting at the performance phase.

3. Assign parts. The chapter breaks do not always make appropriate beginning and ending points. I recommend these divisions: 1:1–13; 1:14–45; 2:1–3:6; 3:7–35; 4:1–34; 4:35–5:43; 6:1–32; 6:33–53;

7:1–23; 7:24–8:26; 8:27–9:13; 9:14–50; 10:1–31; 10:32–52; 11:1–25; 11:27–12:17; 12:18–44; 13:1–37; 14:1–31; 14:32–72; 15:1–32; 15:33–47; 16:1–8. You may wish to have the same reader take the first and final readings (both short) to provide an overall frame for the reading. If you have fewer than twenty-two readers, assign readers multiple but not adjacent parts as needed.

4. Choose an appropriate date and time for the reading. Our parish has been reading one of the Gospels through on the Tuesday of Holy Week for over a decade. Since the Gospel of Mark has been described as a passion story with a long introduction, this setting has worked well for us. Choose equally well for your community.

5. Choose an appropriate place for the reading and work out the listening and reading positions. If your reading will be taking place in a sanctuary or chapel, you might try reading 1:1–8:21 from the lectern, 8:22–10:52 (the "way" section) from the crossing or central aisle, and 11–16 from the pulpit. Whatever your space, representing these three divisions of the Gospel by different reading positions will underline the movement of the story. Think about any special needs of readers. Most will find it easier to read from a book on a stand; a music stand works in an open space. Will any readers need to hold onto something more stable than a music stand? Will any need larger type? Check for adequate lighting on the text. Will any readers need a small stool or step to reach the lectern? Are there stairs or steps that present a problem for anyone? How can listeners be made more comfortable for a long sit? (We spread out so that everyone can freely shift positions.)

6. Encourage each reader to prepare by reading his or her portion aloud. The most frequent problems to avoid are reading too fast or reading too softly. It should not be necessary to practice as an entire group, although individual readers may wish to seek each other out as trial listeners. Remind all readers that this is not an oratorical contest but a shared experience. Some mispronounced words and missed phrases will not "ruin" what you are doing; they will simply be reminders of our shared humanity and the dynamic nature of storytelling.

7. Encourage additional listeners to come for the reading. Use your church bulletin, newsletter, Web page, and/or announcement time

to offer an invitation. At our first reading, everyone in the "audience" was also a reader, but the circle has continued to broaden as others hear of our experience together.

8. Make arrangements for child care as appropriate for your group. Sitting still for an hour and a half is not good news for most young children—or for the adults and young people around them.

AT THE TIME OF THE READING

1. Have someone welcome the readers and listeners with a *brief* description of what will happen and a few tips on what to listen for. If you have arranged for different reading positions, explain why. Perhaps the Echoes section of this guide would be helpful in organizing some introductory comments, especially if there are listeners who have not been a part of a study of Mark. The prayers repeated in the Echoes section are invocations appropriate for those preparing to hear a reading of Mark's Gospel.

2. Encourage everyone to listen—attentively listen—rather than following along in the text. As I have said in my parish, "The text you have with you always, and you can read it whenever you want. Listening is not always a possibility. It is the mystery that is given now. Have ears to hear." Provide each reader with a list of all the readers in their assigned order so that readers can know when it is their turn without having to follow along in the text.

3. Avoid adding too much in the way of introduction, since the reading itself will likely take about an hour and a half. But be sure to announce in the beginning how the reading will close—perhaps, "After the reading, please keep silence and leave in silence when you wish."

4. If your church uses a liturgical formula for introducing Scripture, have the first reader only use it, adapting it as necessary. For example, not "A reading from the Gospel of Mark" but "A reading of the Gospel of Mark." Likewise, have the last reader only (perhaps the same person) use any liturgical closing. For example, Reader (having paused after completing 16:8): "The Word of the Lord." All: "Thanks be to God." In any case, let silence follow, while all ponder the silence of the women fleeing the empty tomb.

An Additional Note on Group Readings

A group reading of the Gospel of Mark is a wonderful gift for a community to give itself. While a dramatic presentation by a single person offers a unity and power all its own, we have found that a shared reading within a community of persons known to each other can bring an unmatched depth. Many readers have "lived in" their reading so fully in preparation that their presentations are moving for all who hear. And there are many voices to hear—many life experiences that are brought to the story and reflected in distinctive understandings. As you hear the story, you hear the storytellers. I suspect this has been happening since the beginning of Mark's Gospel. Perhaps it was in such storytelling within his community that Mark discovered that the "good news" is always beginning.